The Pocket Book of
FRUIT & NUT COOKING

The Pocket Book of
FRUIT & NUT COOKING

Gwyneth Ashmore

Evans Brothers Limited London

Published by
Evans Brothers Limited
Montague House
Russell Square, London WC1B 5BX

Text © Gwyneth Ashmore 1981
Illustrations © Evans Brothers Limited 1981
First published 1981

Drawings by Trevor Aldus

**British Library Cataloguing in Publication
Data**
Ashmore, Gwyneth
    The pocket book of fruit and nut cooking.
    1. Cookery (Fruit)
    2. Cookery (Nuts)
    641.6'4   TX811

ISBN 0-237-45547-1

Printed in Great Britain by Clark Constable Ltd,
Edinburgh
PRA 7110

CONTENTS

INTRODUCTION

When I first went to live abroad I had no idea how to cook; I did not know what good food looked or tasted like. That was in 1950, and ten years of rationing had not been conducive to learning how to cook or to enjoy eating; one ate to live. I lived for seven years in Yugoslavia altogether, and it was there, during my first stay (1950 to 1953), that I discovered how interesting cooking could be. I made many Yugoslav friends (even in those difficult days) and they gave me their beautiful regional recipes and taught me how to cook them. The next country I lived in, Finland, had quite different cooking traditions; so did Kenya, Israel and Switzerland, but there, too, I made friends, and they gave me their recipes and showed me how to make them. They frequently passed me on to their friends in other parts of their country. Many of these friends were not indigenous people; they were Greeks, Americans, Spaniards, Germans, Indians, Romanians, to mention but a few.

By the time I went to live in Finland, I was confident enough to do all the catering and cooking for the official entertaining my husband and I had to do, and by the time I went to Switzerland, twenty years later, I was a professional amateur chef. In fact, I found myself giving lessons and lectures on cooking for entertaining after a local journalist had written a flattering article in a Zurich newspaper. (She had attended a reception I had catered for at a press show of the opening of a British Council Arts Exhibition.) I learnt a lot about Swiss cooking by picking my pupils' brains and practising on our guests in the evening.

When I finally returned to England, a few years ago, a friend I had met in Finland (a health food fanatic) aroused my interest in the use of fruit and nuts in cooking. As I looked through the many recipes I had collected over the years I was amazed at how many of them used fruit and nuts, and I started experimenting with these recipes which so many people in so many countries had given me. After all, old English cooking used indigenous fruits and nuts, apples, plums, medlars, quinces, walnuts, hazelnuts, chestnuts and soft fruits. Nowadays we seem to have forgotten the use of these fruits in savoury dishes, and we use them mostly with large quantities of white sugar as puddings. Since we now have many more fruits and nuts available, it's time, I think, we became more adventurous and went back to using them to enhance our meat and fish dishes, even as substitutes for meat and fish. Old English recipes do not, of course, include these imported fruits and nuts, but we can use the cooking traditions of the countries where they grow. This is why I wrote this book.

Weights and measures

The following table is approximate. 1oz = 28.352 grammes but it is simpler to say 1oz = 30 grammes.

$$15g = \frac{1}{2}oz$$
$$30g = 1oz$$
$$60g = 2oz$$
$$75g = 2\frac{1}{2}oz$$
$$100g = 3\frac{1}{2}oz$$
$$500g = 1lb\ 1\frac{1}{2}oz$$

$$1\ litre = 1\frac{3}{4}\ pints$$
$$1\ decilitre\ (dcl) = 3\ to\ 4fl.\ oz - approx.\ one\ wineglass$$
$$3dcl = \frac{1}{2}\ pint$$

Temperatures

°C	°F	Gas regulo mark	
105	225	$\frac{1}{4}$	very cool
120	250	$\frac{1}{2}$	very cool
135	275	1	cool
150	300	2	cool
160	325	3	warm
175	350	4	moderate
190	375	5	fairly hot
205	400	6	hot
220	425	7	hot
230	450	8	very hot
245	475	9	very hot

SOUPS

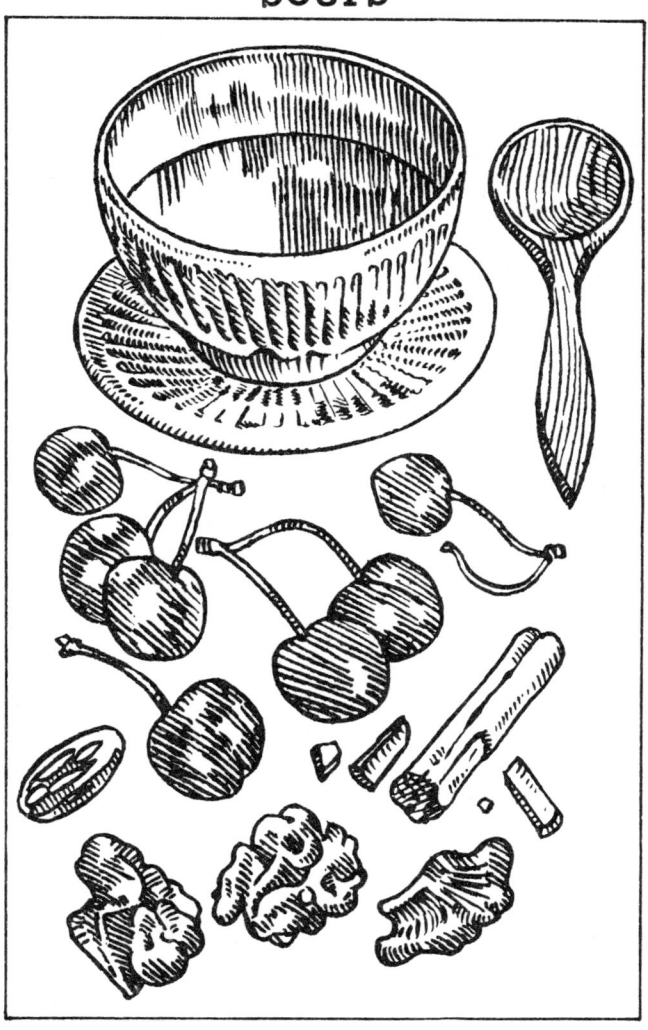

Fish soup

500g fish (whiting, cod, etc.)
2 onions
3 large cloves of garlic, sliced thinly
1 red pepper, with seeds removed and flesh cut into strips
4 tomatoes, skinned (the easiest way to do this is to put the tomatoes in boiling water for a few minutes; then remove the skins)
1 tablespoon chopped parsley
6dcl fish stock made from the bones, head, etc. of the fish, plus an onion, a carrot, mixed herbs
100g almonds and hazelnuts, chopped
Salt, pepper, flour, oil

Cut the fish into pieces, flour them and fry them in oil till a light golden brown colour. Remove the fish to a dish and fry the onion, garlic, red pepper and tomatoes in the oil where the fish was fried, till the vegetables are soft. Then add the parsley and fry for another minute. Bring the stock to the boil and add the nuts and all the fried ingredients, including the fish. Simmer till the fish is cooked and the liquid reduced a little.

Cold melon soup

1 clove garlic
100g ground almonds
2 tablespoons oil (sesame seed oil is best)
1 tablespoon cider vinegar
1 ripe melon
6dcl yoghurt
Salt and pepper
Pinch of nutmeg

Crush the garlic with salt, mix with the ground almonds, oil and vinegar. Remove the melon skin and pips, and chop the fruit into cubes about 2cm square. Mix the yoghurt with the garlic, almond mixture, pepper and nutmeg and then mix in the melon cubes. Chill and serve cold.

Yoghurt soup, cold

1½dcl yoghurt
1 cucumber chopped into
  small pieces
100g seedless raisins
3 tablespoons chopped
  chives

1 tablespoon chopped fresh
  dill, if available. If not
  available, use chopped
  fennel leaves
Salt, pepper

Beat the yoghurt and then add the cucumber, raisins, salt and pepper to taste, and the chopped chives and dill. Serve cold.

Avocado soup, cold

2 large avocados
9dcl white stock
6dcl yoghurt

1 large clove garlic
Salt, pepper

Remove the skins and stones from the avocados, blend the flesh with the stock and yoghurt, add the garlic clove crushed in salt, and salt and pepper to taste. Serve cold.

Cold oriental soup

250g almonds
240g cooked haricot beans
3 small cloves garlic
1½dcl olive oil (any
  vegetable oil will do)

Water as needed
75g dried wholewheat
  breadcrumbs
Salt, pepper

Skin the almonds and grind them. Put the haricot beans through a mouli and mash them with the almonds. Mash the garlic with a little salt and mix with the beans and almonds. Add the oil slowly, as one does for mayonnaise, and stir till the mixture is smooth. Then add enough cold water to make a thinnish soup, stir in the breadcrumbs and cool. Serve very cold.

Grape soup with garlic

4 garlic cloves
50g ground almonds
75g wholewheat
   breadcrumbs
2 tablespoons olive oil

1 tablespoon cider vinegar
6dcl chicken or veal stock
500g seeded grapes
Salt

Pound the garlic and almonds together with the bread-crumbs. Add a little salt, then mix the oil in slowly, followed by the vinegar. Then stir in the stock, add the grapes and put in the refrigerator. Serve chilled.

Curried apple soup

1 large chopped onion
2 tablespoons oil
1 teaspoon curry powder
6dcl white stock (veal stock
   is best)
The yolks of 2 eggs
1dcl cream

150g eating apples
The juice of 1 lemon
1 tablespoon chopped
   lemon balm
1 coffeespoon grated lemon
   rind

Cook the onion in the oil till it is soft and a pale golden colour. Add the curry powder and fry slowly for about 4 minutes, then add the stock, mix well and bring to the boil. Reduce the heat and simmer for 10 minutes. Remove the pan from the heat. Mix the egg yolks with the cream and add to the soup; beat in well.

Reserve two apples, peel and core the remaining apples and put into a blender with some of the soup; blend until smooth, then mix with the rest of the soup. Put into a double boiler and mix over boiling water till the soup thickens. Cool. Dice the remaining cored, peeled apples and pour the lemon juice over them. Scatter the lemon rind and chopped lemon balm over the soup before serving, and serve the diced apples as a garnish.

The soup can also be served hot, without the apple garnish.

Finnish cold fruit soup

250g dried apricots
250g prunes
100g dried pears
1 litre water
3 large apples, cored and
cut into cubes

100g sugar
4cm piece of stick
cinnamon
1 heaped tablespoon
cornflour
Sour cream

Soak the dried fruit for 12 hours in the water. Put the soaked fruit and water in a pan with the apples, sugar and cinnamon. Simmer till the fruit is cooked, then strain. Stone the prunes and remove the cinnamon. Mix the cornflour with a little water, then add it to the fruit water, heat and thicken. Simmer for 5 minutes, add the fruit and mix well in. Allow to get cold, and serve with sour cream.

Slovene apple soup

2kg sour apples, pipped,
cored and (if preferred)
skinned
The peel of 1 small lemon,
grated
4cm piece of stick
cinnamon and 6 cloves,
ground together

Sugar to taste (depending
on the sweetness of the
apples)
5dcl white wine
Water as needed
Salt, pepper
Chopped walnuts to
garnish

Cook the apples in a little water with the lemon rind, cinnamon and cloves and sugar. When they are cooked, put through a food mill or blend. Add the wine and enough water to make the consistency of thin cream. Season and add more sugar if necessary. Chill and serve with chopped walnuts scattered over the soup.

Hot apple soup

500g apples
2dcl white wine
The grated rind of 1 lemon
30g brown sugar
2 litres water

250g sultanas
250g currants
30g butter
30g flour

Cut the apples into pieces and cook them slowly with the wine, lemon rind and sugar. Sieve the cooked apples, put in a large pan and add the currants, sultanas and water. Blend the butter and the flour. Bring the apple soup to boiling point, then add the butter and flour mixture in small pieces to the simmering soup, mix together till the soup thickens and is smooth.

Almond cream soup

100g finely chopped
   almonds
5dcl white stock
1 small onion, sliced
2 celery stalks, cut into
   small pieces

1 tablespoon butter
1 tablespoon flour
3dcl milk
1dcl sour cream
Salt, pepper

Put the almonds into a pan with the stock, onion and celery. Bring to the boil and simmer together for about 20 minutes. Put through a sieve or into a blender.

Combine the butter with the flour and make into little pieces the size of a hazelnut. Put the stock back into the pan, if necessary add stock or water to make 5dcl, and add the butter/flour pieces to the simmering stock, stirring till it thickens. Then add the milk, cream and salt and pepper to taste, bring to boiling point and serve at once.

Apricot soup

250g apricots
30g brown sugar (or more, depending on the ripeness of the fruit)

1 litre water
30g butter
30g flour
The juice of 1 lemon

Stone the apricots and put them with the sugar in the water; bring to boiling point. Simmer for about three-quarters of an hour. Sieve the fruit, or put it through a food mill, or blend in a liquidizer.

Mix the butter with the flour. Reheat the fruit purée and put the butter and flour mixture in little pieces into the simmering soup. Stir till the butter and flour are blended in and the soup thickens, pour the lemon juice into the soup and serve.

Cherry soup

500g cherries
3dcl red wine
2dcl hot water
1 piece of stick cinnamon, about 1cm long

The peel of ½ a lemon, grated
1 teaspoon cornflour

Stone the cherries, crush the cherry stones and put the stones into a pan with the wine. Bring to the boil and simmer for about 10 minutes, then strain through a very fine sieve. Put the cherries into a pan with the hot water, cinnamon, and lemon peel. Cook fast for about 10 minutes, then sieve or pulp in a blender. Put back into the pan, add the wine and bring to the boil, then add the cornflour mixed with a little water. Mix well into the soup, reheat, add a little sugar if necessary, and serve.

Chestnut soup

6dcl white stock
300g shelled chestnuts
1 onion, sliced
½ coffeespoon celery salt

1 tablespoon butter
1 dessertspoon flour
3dcl single cream

Put the stock, chestnuts, onion and celery salt into a pan.
Bring to the boil and simmer till the chestnuts are soft.
Either put into a blender or through a mouli. Cook the
flour in the butter till it is a golden brown colour, add the
stock, little by little, and stir till smooth. Add the cream,
reheat to boiling point, add more salt, if necessary, and
serve.

EGGS

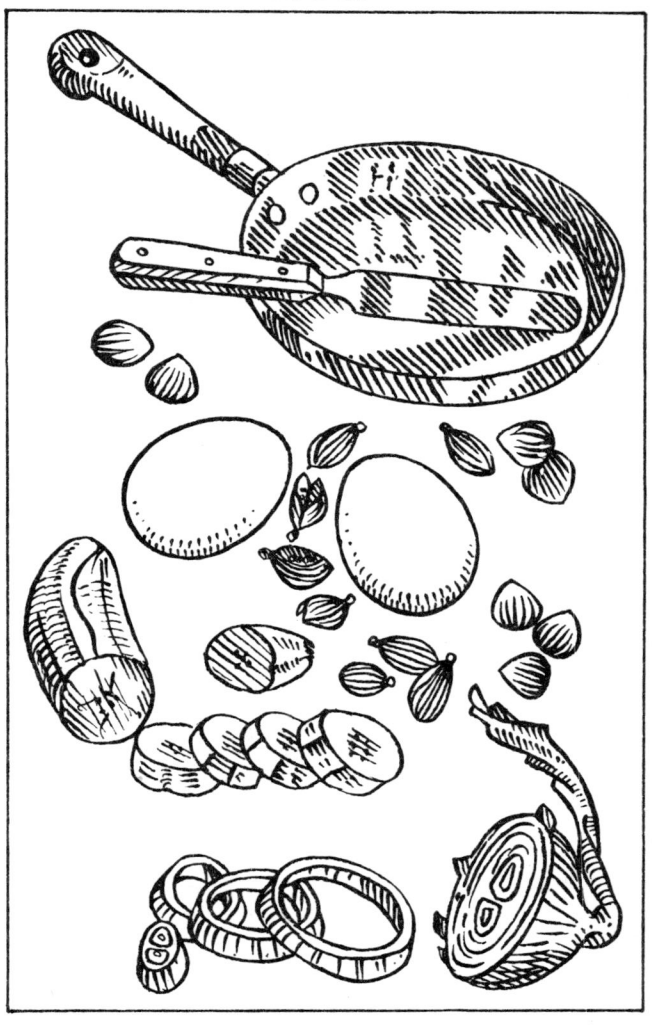

Fried Cuban eggs

2 chopped onions
2 garlic cloves, mashed
4 tablespoons oil
150g rice
6dcl white stock
4 ripe bananas

Brown sugar to taste
1dcl lemon juice
4 eggs
Oil to fry the eggs in
Salt, freshly ground pepper

Cook the onion and garlic in 2 tablespoons of oil to a golden brown colour. Add the rice and cook for 4 minutes. Heat the stock and add it to the rice, bring to the boil, reduce the heat and simmer till the rice is cooked – do not overcook.

Skin the bananas, cut them lengthwise, then in halves, and fry them in the remaining oil; add a little salt and pepper, and sugar if liked, then pour the lemon juice over. Keep hot while the eggs are fried. Serve the eggs and bananas on top of the rice.

If liked, serve this with a spicy sauce.

Banana omelette

60g butter
2 ripe bananas
¼ coffeespoon ground nutmeg
¼ coffeespoon ground cinnamon

¼ coffeespoon ground cardamom seeds
Salt, pepper
2 eggs

Melt 30g of the butter in a pan, then put the peeled, sliced bananas into it with the spices and a little salt and pepper. Cook till the banana is soft. Separate the eggs. Beat the whites until stiff; beat the yolks and fold the whites into the yolks. Heat the remaining butter in a frying pan; when it is hot, pour the eggs into the pan. When they begin to set, cover the omelette with the banana, fold it over and serve at once.

19

Nut omelette

150g hazelnuts, chopped
　　small
¼ coffeespoon nutmeg
¼ coffeespoon ground
　　cloves

Salt, pepper
3 eggs
30g butter

Mix the nuts with the spices, salt and pepper. Separate the eggs. Beat the egg yolks a little and mix with the nuts. Beat the egg whites stiff and mix the nuts and yolks into them. Melt the butter in a frying pan and when it is hot put the egg mixture into it. When the omelette begins to set, fold over, fry a minute or two more, and serve.

Spiced hard-boiled eggs

100g skinned almonds
6 hard-boiled eggs
1 tablespoon lemon juice
1 tablespoon garlic salt
1 level teaspoon turmeric
2dcl yoghurt
½dcl thick cream
1 coffeespoon kolonji (wild
　　black onion seeds)

50g roasted ground poppy
　　seeds
1 ground bay leaf
1 coffeespoon (or less) chilli
　　pepper
50g sesame seeds
½ coffeespoon (or less) salt

Cut the almonds into slivers and insert into the eggs. Make a few cuts into the white part of the eggs. Mix the lemon juice, garlic salt and turmeric together and sprinkle over the eggs. Put the yoghurt and cream into a saucepan and put over a low heat. When hot, add the kolonji, poppy seeds, bay leaf, chilli pepper, sesame seeds and salt. Cook till the mixture thickens, moisten with a little water, add the eggs and heat them in the sauce. Serve with rice.

FISH

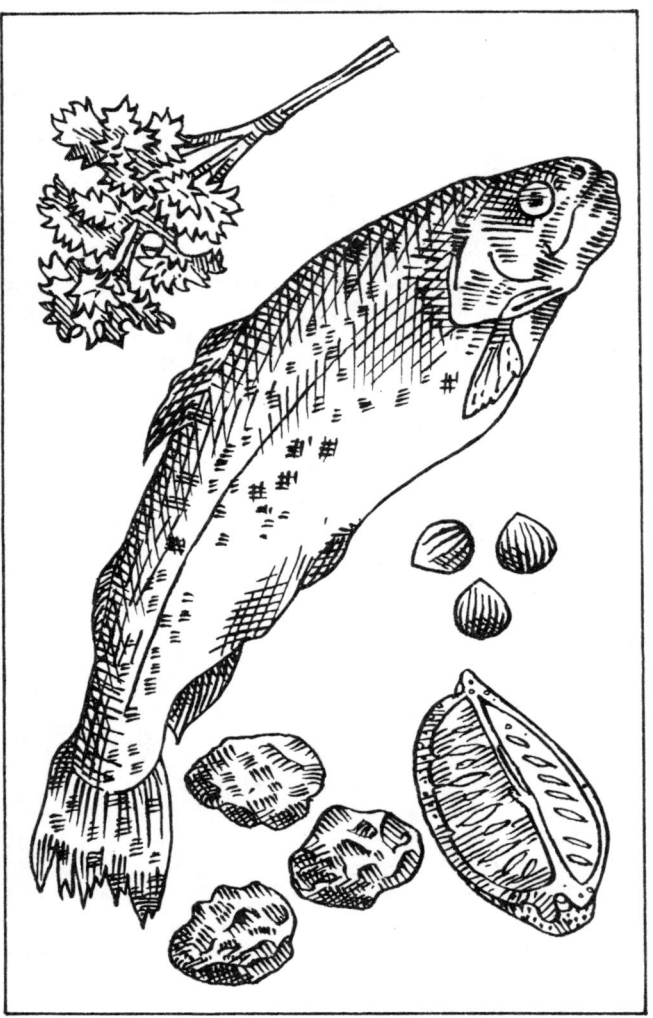

Fish and vegetable stew with lemon

1kg fish (e.g. cod, haddock),
   whole or in large pieces
½ cucumber
4 large tomatoes, skinned
½dcl vegetable oil
2 onions, chopped small
4 garlic cloves (less if
   preferred), crushed in salt

1 bay leaf, crushed or
   ground
1 tablespoon chopped
   parsley
The juice of 1 large lemon
Salt, pepper

Oil an ovenproof dish and put the fish into it. Slice the cucumber and tomatoes and place over the fish. Mix the oil, chopped onions, garlic, bay leaf, parsley and lemon together. Add a little pepper and salt and pour the mixture over the fish, tomato and cucumber. Bake in a moderately hot oven till cooked (about an hour).

Fish with prune sauce

1 large freshwater fish such
   as carp
4dcl apple vinegar
7dcl water
1 sliced carrot
2 celery stalks

1 large onion, thinly sliced
1 parsnip, thinly sliced
1 clove garlic
5 cloves
2cm green ginger
Salt, pepper

Prune sauce
250gm cooked prunes
100g chopped hazelnuts
100g raisins

The juice and grated rind of
   ½ a lemon
25g butter

Cut the fish into serving pieces. Put all the ingredients except the fish, and those for the sauce, into a pan and heat. When boiling point is reached, reduce heat and simmer for about 30 minutes. Then add the fish and simmer for another 30 minutes. Remove the fish and bone it, put it into a dish and keep warm. Strain and reserve the stock for the sauce.

To make the sauce, remove the stones from the prunes. Cut the prunes into pieces and mix with the nuts, lemon rind and juice, raisins and butter, then add the mixture to the fish stock. Cook till the stock is reduced by half. Pour over the fish and serve, hot or cold.

Lemon fish pie

100g dried brown
  breadcrumbs
4 garlic cloves, shredded
1 tablespoon oil plus a little
  more for the topping
The juice of 2 lemons

The grated rind of 1 lemon
Salt, pepper
1kg white fish such as
  whiting, cod, etc.
  (skinned and boned)

Mix the breadcrumbs and garlic, tablespoon of oil, salt and pepper with the lemon juice and lemon peel. Oil an ovenproof dish and put a layer of the breadcrumb mixture on the bottom. Cover with a layer of fish, then one of crumbs, then one of fish and so on till everything is used up, finishing with a layer of crumbs. Moisten the top with a little more oil and bake in a moderately hot oven for about three-quarters of an hour.

Whiting with prunes

12 large prunes, presoaked
  and stoned
4 tablespoons cooked brown
  rice
2 tablespoons lemon balm
Salt, pepper

4 whiting or similar fish,
  cleaned
60g butter
6dcl sour cream (yoghurt
  will do)

Mix the prunes, chopped into small pieces, rice, lemon balm, salt and pepper together and stuff the fish with the mixture. Sew up the opening. Put the fish into an oven dish, dab with pieces of butter, pour the sour cream or yoghurt over the fish and bake for about 45 minutes.

Grilled fish with lemon butter sauce

The juice of 1 lemon
1dcl melted butter
4 fish for grilling
(mackerel, herring, etc.)
2 teaspoons chopped
tarragon

2 teaspoons chopped fennel
leaves
2 dessertspoons chopped
parsley
Salt, pepper

Butter sauce
2dcl melted butter
Juice of 1½ lemons

3 tablespoons chopped
tarragon

Mix the lemon juice with the melted butter and moisten the fish with some of it. Salt and pepper the fish. Mix the tarragon with the fennel and parsley and put inside the fish. Grill the fish, basting with the remaining lemon juice and butter.

Make the sauce by mixing the butter with the tarragon and lemon juice. Remove the grilled fish to a serving dish, scrape up the pan juices and put with the fish. Serve the sauce separately.

Lake Ohrid trout

4 trout, cleaned
300g prunes
100g chopped parsley
3 cloves garlic, chopped
very small
1½dcl white wine

4 eggs
The juice of 1 lemon and 1
lemon cut into wedges for
garnish
3dcl oil

Wash the trout and dry them; sprinkle with salt and pepper. Remove the stones from the prunes. Make little incisions in the trout and put a half prune in each hole. Chop up the remaining prunes and stuff the trout with them. Oil an oven dish, scatter the parsley and garlic over it, put the fish in the dish, pour the wine over and bake in a hot oven, basting from time to time. Remove the fish to a serving dish and keep warm.

Beat the eggs and lemon juice together, then add the oil, little by little. Mix with the pan juices and heat till the sauce thickens, add salt and pepper (if necessary), pour over the trout and serve.

Lemon with trout

4 trout
Wholewheat flour, as
  needed
Salt, pepper
100g butter, or more, to
  taste
1 teaspoon chopped fennel
  leaves

2 large cloves garlic
  (optional)
1 heaped tablespoon
  chopped parsley
The juice of 2 large lemons

Clean the trout, dry them and roll them in the flour with a little salt and pepper. Put some butter into the grill pan, lay the fish on top and put more butter on top of the fish. Grill till the fish are brown and cooked, turning over to brown both sides. This will take about 20 minutes, depending on the size of the trout. When cooked, remove to a serving dish and keep hot.

Fry the fennel, garlic and parsley in the pan juices for a few minutes, add lemon juice and mix well. Pour over the fish and serve.

Fish in lemon skins

4 large lemons
200g cooked fish
2 tablespoons mayonnaise

2 tablespoons lemon juice
1 hard-boiled egg

Cut the lemons in half, remove their flesh and pith. Flake the fish, add the mayonnaise and lemon juice and fill the lemon shells with the mixture. Chop the hard-boiled egg and put on top of the stuffed lemon shells. Serve with a green salad.

Skate with orange

500g skate
Stock or water to cook the skate (approx. 1 litre)
1 bay leaf, 2 large sprigs of parsley, a few fennel leaves, some lemon balm
100g chopped onion
The juice of ½ lemon
2 teaspoons salt
Black pepper

For the sauce
3 oranges
2 onions
30g butter
1 tablespoon chopped parsley
1 teaspoon chopped fennel
Salt, pepper

Prepare the sauce first. Peel and slice two of the oranges, squeeze the juice from the third. Cook the onions, sliced thinly, in about half the butter, till soft and golden. Put the rest of the butter into the pan with the onions and fry the orange slices in it for a few minutes, add the juice of the third orange and the herbs, salt and pepper. Set aside while you prepare the skate.

Put the skate into the heated fish stock or water, with the herbs, onion, lemon juice, salt and pepper, bring to the boil, reduce heat and simmer for 30 minutes. Drain the fish, remove the skin, cut into pieces and keep hot.

Reheat the sauce to boiling point, pour over the skate and serve.

Fillets of fish cooked in apple juice

4 plaice fillets
1 bay leaf
Salt, pepper
3dcl apple juice

1 tablespoon chopped parsley
1 dessertspoon lemon balm (if available) chopped

Put the fish in an oven dish with the bay leaf, salt and pepper. Heat the apple juice and pour over the fish. Cover with foil and cook in a hot oven for about 20 minutes. Scatter the herbs over the fish and serve.

Grape juice can be used instead of apple in this recipe.

Yugoslav carp

1kg carp
2 lemons
250g onions
750g potatoes
Sunflower oil, flour as
  needed

Salt, pepper
1 clove garlic
1dcl cream

Wash and clean the carp, cut it into pieces about 2cm thick, salt them and sprinkle the juice of 1 lemon over them. Leave for an hour.

Slice the onions and potatoes thinly. Oil an ovenproof dish (earthenware is best) and put a layer of potatoes over the bottom; sprinkle with a little salt and pepper. Top this with the onions, salted and peppered, then cover this layer with the remaining potatoes. Mix about 1dcl of oil with the juice of the other lemon and pour over the top. Bake in a hot oven for about 30 minutes.

While the potatoes and onions are cooking, fry the garlic, thinly sliced, in some oil till pale golden. Dip each piece of carp in a little flour and fry in the same pan till golden brown. Put the pieces of carp on top of the vegetables, pour the cream over the top and bake for about 20 minutes.

Trout with bananas

4 trout
4 bananas
Flour, salt, pepper

150g butter
The juice of 1 lemon
2 oranges

Remove the heads and backbones from the trout. Skin the bananas, roll them in flour, put one banana in each trout and tie up the fish. Salt and pepper the fish, roll them in flour and fry in hot butter till brown and cooked. Put into a hot serving dish.

Mix the lemon juice with the pan juices and pour over the fish. Have ready the oranges, peeled, sliced and heated a little, to serve as a garnish with the trout.

Boiled mackerel with gooseberry sauce

4 fresh mackerel, cleaned
  and with heads removed

Gooseberry sauce

3dcl gooseberries
1 tablespoon cooked sorrel
  leaves, chopped finely
  (spinach will do if you
  cannot get sorrel)

30g butter
30g brown sugar
A little ground nutmeg
Salt

Poach the mackerel in salted water for about 20 minutes
(depending on the size). Drain and serve with the
gooseberry sauce made as follows.

Boil the gooseberries in a little water till soft and put
through a food mill, or blend. Add the chopped sorrel
leaves, butter, sugar, nutmeg and salt to taste. Reheat and
serve.

Fish with rhubarb

250g rhubarb (not forced
  rhubarb)
1 medium sized onion,
  chopped small
2 dessertspoons of ground
  coriander
¼ teaspoon ground black
  pepper
1 medium sized red pepper,
  chopped very small

1 medium sized green
  pepper, chopped small
500g filleted fish
1dcl oil
Salt
¼ coffeespoon ground
  nutmeg
¼ coffeespoon ground
  cardamom seeds

Cook the rhubarb (with a little sugar if liked) in an
earthenware pot with a well fitting lid and no water in the
oven till soft. Sieve or put into a blender to make a purée.

Mix the chopped onion with the coriander, black pepper,
red and green peppers and rub over the fish fillets. Heat
the oil and put the fish into it, lower the heat, add salt,

nutmeg, cardamom and rhubarb purée. Cover the pan and cook till the fish is done, about 15 minutes, depending on the size and thickness of the fillets.

Crab with peaches

4 fresh peaches
250g crabmeat
1½dcl sour cream (fresh
  cream will do)

Salt, pepper

Slice the top off each peach and remove the stones. Remove some of the flesh inside the fruit to make a space for the filling. Chop the crabmeat finely and mix with the fruit removed from the peaches, and the cream. Season the mixture with salt and pepper and stuff it back into the peaches. Chill before serving.

Lemon with mussels

1 litre mussels
70g butter
1 onion, chopped small
1 carrot, chopped small
1 garlic clove mashed in
  salt
Salt, pepper

¼ teaspoon grated nutmeg
1 tablespoon chopped
  parsley
¼ teaspoon chopped thyme
1 bay leaf
The juice of 5 lemons
25g flour

Wash the mussels and clean them. Put 30g of butter into a pan, add the onion and carrot, garlic, salt, pepper and nutmeg. When the onion and carrot are soft, add the herbs and lemon juice and simmer together for a few minutes. Put the mussels in the pan and cook over a high heat, shaking the pan till the mussel shells open. Drain off the liquid and reserve it. Remove the mussels from their shells and keep hot.

Heat the remaining butter and brown the flour in it. Add the liquid from the cooked mussels, simmer for a few minutes, pour the sauce over the mussels and serve.

Kalamari (squid)

1kg kalamari
2 level tablespoons salt
2dcl olive oil
1½dcl white wine
3 medium sized tomatoes,
  peeled and chopped small

1 tablespoon chopped
  parsley
Pepper
Juice and grated peel of 1
  lemon

Clean the squid, rub well with salt, wash and drain. Heat
the oil, sauté the squid, then add the wine, tomatoes,
parsley and pepper and cook on a low heat till the squid is
tender and the juices thick. This will take about 45
minutes. Then add the lemon juice and grated lemon peel
and allow to cool. Serve cold.

Greek octopus

1 octopus (about 500g)
1 tablespoon salt
1½dcl olive oil
¾dcl white wine
2 medium sized tomatoes,
  peeled and chopped small

1 dessertspoon chopped
  parsley
Pepper to taste
1 lemon

Clean the octopus well, beat it to soften the flesh, rub with
salt, then wash and drain.

Heat the oil and sauté the octopus on all sides. Add the
wine, tomatoes, parsley and pepper. Bring to the boil,
reduce heat and simmer with a tight fitting lid till the
flesh is tender and the sauce thick. It will take about 3
hours to cook. Cool, adjust the seasoning and serve with
lemon wedges or with the juice of the lemon poured over it.

Crab, pineapple and grapefruit salad

2 teaspoons gelatine
1dcl grapefruit juice
1 tablespoon apple vinegar
1½dcl thick mayonnaise

400g crabmeat
150g mashed grapefruit
150g chopped pineapple

Melt the gelatine over hot water with the grapefruit juice.
When melted, add the vinegar. Mix this, drop by drop, into
the mayonnaise, beating well. Mix the crabmeat with the
grapefruit and pineapple, then mix into the mayonnaise.
Put into a serving dish and chill.

Grapefruit salad

4 grapefruit
8 spring onions
4 stalks of celery
4 or more ripe green olives

Salad dressing:
olive oil, lemon juice, salt,
    pepper

Peel the grapefruit and remove the fruit sections. Cut the spring onions into small pieces, including the green part. Cut the celery into chunks, mix together and then mix in the salad dressing. Garnish with the olives.

Peach salad

4 large ripe peaches
2 stalks celery
Salad dressing made from:
    sunflower oil, fresh lime
    juice (if not available use
    lemon juice), celery salt,
    a little sugar if liked

1dcl chopped nuts
Green salad

Cut the peaches in half and remove the stones. Chop the celery and nuts, moisten with a little of the dressing and fill the peach centres with the mixture. Prepare the green salad, mix with the dressing, arrange in a shallow bowl, top with the peach halves.

Pear salad

6 ripe pears
1 large bunch watercress

Salad dressing:
1½dcl yoghurt, 2
    tablespoons of lemon
    juice, salt, pepper

Core the pears and cut into pieces (do not remove the skins). Mix the pear pieces with the cleaned watercress and salad dressing.

Orange salad

6 large oranges
1 large bunch of
watercress, cleaned

Salad dressing:
sunflower oil, cider
vinegar, chopped chives,
salt and pepper

Peel the oranges, remove the fruit sections, mix with the watercress and salad dressing.

Cherry salad

1½kg firm ripe cherries
1 litre white wine vinegar
2 cloves
1 coffeespoon of chopped
peppermint leaves

1 piece stick cinnamon
about 6cm long
¼ teaspoon freshly grated
nutmeg
200g sugar

Wash the cherries and then dry them. Put the vinegar into a deep pan, add the herbs, spices and sugar and bring to the boil. Simmer for about half an hour, cool and then pour over the cherries. Put into a container, cover and leave in a cool place for ten days. Serve with smoked meat or fish.

Port Royal salad

250g cooked small potatoes,
sliced
250g cored eating apples,
sliced
250g French beans cooked
and cut into pieces

4dcl good mayonnaise
1 lettuce, cleaned and cut
in quarters
4 hard boiled eggs, cut in
quarters

Mix the potatoes, apples and beans together on a serving dish, and add the mayonnaise. Surround the vegetable salad with lettuce, and put the egg quarters on top.

Avocado pear salad

4 large ripe avocado pears
    (It is essential that the
    avocados are ripe. They
    should be soft to the
    touch. Unripe avocados
    taste of nothing.)

1 Remove the stone from the avocados, and if they are not to be eaten at once spread a little lemon juice over the flesh; this will prevent it discolouring. Put the salad dressing made from olive oil, garlic, salt and cider vinegar into the centre and serve.

2 Fill the centre with chopped cucumber moistened with yoghurt mixed with a little lemon juice and olive oil and flavoured with garlic salt and pepper.

Prunes stuffed with cheese

Cook the prunes and cool, remove stones. Fill with a mixture of cream cheese, chopped chives, salt and pepper with a little cream.

Stuffed tomatoes

Remove a slice at the top of the tomato, remove some of the inside pulp and all the seeds. Fill with fresh pineapple chopped very small and mixed with freshly chopped walnuts in a mayonnaise sauce. Serve on a lettuce salad.

Stuffed peaches

Halve the peaches and remove the stones. Fill with cream cheese flavoured with chopped fresh tarragon and chopped chives, moistened with a little yoghurt or cream.

Greek chick pea salad

500g chick peas
½ teaspoon baking powder
½ cup tahini (sesame seed
    paste) – about 1½dcl
2 lemons
½ cup olive oil (1½dcl)

Salt, pepper
2 large garlic cloves,
    crushed
2 tablespoons chopped
    parsley

Cover the chick peas with water, add the baking powder and soak overnight. In the morning drain them, wash, cover with water and cook gently for two hours or till they are soft. Drain them and sieve them or put them through a food mill. Beat the tahini with 2 tablespoons of water till smooth. Extract the juice from the lemons. Add the tahini and lemon juice alternately to the chick peas with the olive oil, then add salt, pepper and garlic and chill. Sprinkle with chopped parsley before serving.

Apple and cheese salad

Eating apples
Cream cheese
Chopped chives

Core the apples and slice them (do not remove the skin). Spread the cream cheese thickly over the slices, scatter the chopped chives over the top.

Carrot salad

4 large carrots
The juice of 1 lemon
Grated rind of ½ a lemon

Salt, pepper,
2 tablespoons of olive oil

Grate the carrots into a bowl, add the lemon juice and let stand for half an hour. Then add the oil, lemon rind, salt and pepper.

Cabbage, apple, celery and mint salad

1 small cabbage
4 celery stalks
4 sweet apples
2 dessertspoons of chopped
  mint

Salad dressing:
olive oil, cider vinegar, salt
  and pepper

Shred the cabbage, chop the celery, core the apples and slice thinly, mix together with the mint. Mix with the salad dressing and serve.

Pineapple, red cabbage and parsley salad

1 small pineapple
1 small red cabbage
2 tablespoons chopped
  parsley

Salad dressing:
sunflower oil, cider
  vinegar, salt, pepper

Skin the pineapple and chop it into small pieces, shred the cabbage, mix together with the parsley and salad dressing.

Banana salad

4 ripe bananas
2dcl chopped nuts (peanuts
  will do)
1 lettuce, cleaned, and with
  the leaves torn in small
  pieces

French dressing:
oil (sesame seed oil is best),
  cider vinegar, salt and
  pepper
2 tangerines, if available,
  peeled and sliced or the
  sections removed from
  their skin

Cut the bananas in quarters, then cut the pieces in half lengthwise. Roll the pieces in the chopped nuts. Mix the lettuce into the French dressing and arrange in a shallow bowl, arranging the banana pieces on top of the salad and decorate with the pieces of tangerine.

Brazilian salad

2dcl white grapes
2dcl chopped fresh
   pineapple
2dcl eating apples, cored
   and chopped small
1dcl black cherries, stoned

2dcl chopped celery
Chopped hazelnuts to taste
Mayonnaise thinned with
   lemon juice
Green salad

Mix the fruits, celery and nuts together, moisten with the lemon mayonnaise and serve on green salad.

MEAT

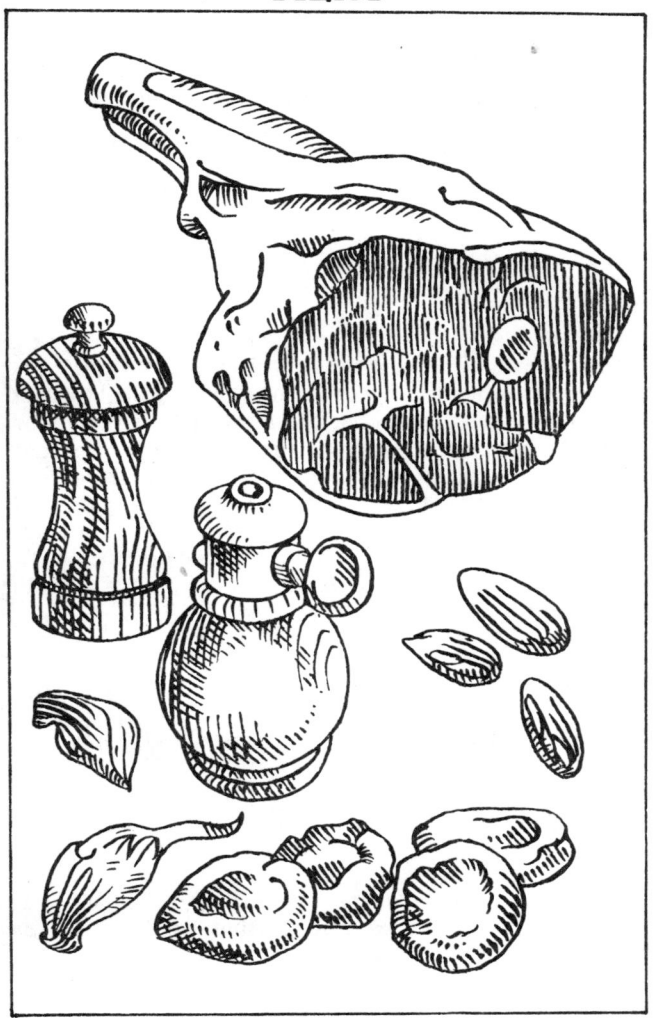

South African beef pie without pastry

500g minced beef
50g white bread
3dcl of milk (sour milk or yoghurt can be used)
2 eggs
1 tablespoon curry powder
2 tablespoons chopped onions
30g butter
2 tablespoons blanched chopped almonds
8 apricots, stoned and chopped (dried can be used)
The juice of one lemon
Salt and pepper
1 dessertspoon chopped parsley
1 teaspoon chopped oregano
1 bay leaf, ground

Soak the bread in the milk, then squeeze to remove excess milk. Beat the eggs and then beat them into the milk. Fry the curry powder and the onions in the butter till soft and golden brown. Mix together the meat and bread, onions, almonds, apricots, lemon juice, salt and pepper and half the milk and egg mixture (or less) and blend well together. Grease a baking dish and fill with the mixture. Bake in a low oven for about an hour then pour over the remaining milk mixture with the ground bay leaf and herbs. Bake for another 20 minutes or more till the topping is set and golden brown.

Courgettes with beef and hazelnut stuffing

500g minced beef
200g chopped onions
80g butter
2 garlic cloves mashed with salt
100g hazelnuts chopped small
Salt and pepper
6 large courgettes
1dcl of tomato juice

Fry the onions in 50g of the butter till they are soft. Add the garlic, fry for another minute, then add the nuts and fry till they are light gold in colour. Add the meat, mix the ingredients together and fry over a low heat for 5 minutes, then season with salt and pepper. Cut the courgettes in halves lengthwise and remove the inner flesh, leaving a good shell of the flesh in the cases. Stuff the meat mixture into the courgettes. Put the remaining 30g of butter in a casserole and fry the outsides of the courgettes in it for about 10 minutes on a very low heat. Heat the tomato juice and, if liked, blend with the removed courgette flesh, add salt and pepper and put into the casserole with the courgettes, cover and cook in a low oven for about 45 minutes. The tomato sauce can be mixed with sour cream before serving.

Braised beef with chestnuts

1½kg joint braising beef
Sunflower oil, or other oil
2 large onions, chopped
4 carrots, sliced thin
2 celery stalks, chopped
   small
200g mushrooms

¼ teaspoon each freshly
   ground black pepper, salt
1 tablespoon chopped
   parsley
250g of chestnuts
1 teaspoon chopped oregano

Marinade
½ litre red wine
3 cloves of garlic mashed
   with salt
1 celery stalk, chopped
1 onion, chopped

1 carrot, chopped
1 bay leaf
1 teaspoon chopped thyme
1 teaspoon chopped lemon
   balm

Mix all the ingredients for the marinade, rub the beef with a little oil and put into the marinade for about 12 hours.

Put some oil into a pan and cook the onions in it till soft, add the carrots and celery and cook another 10 minutes. Add the mushrooms and cook another 5 minutes. Put the vegetables into a casserole, and add the meat. Heat the marinade, strain and pour into the casserole, add salt and pepper to taste and chopped oregano and parsley. Cook in a slow oven for about 3 hours. Have the chestnuts skinned. Add them to the casserole and simmer for about 45 minutes or till they are tender.

Spanish minced beef and fruit

750g minced beef
2 onions sliced thinly
50g butter
2 ripe tomatoes, peeled and chopped small
Salt and freshly ground black pepper to taste
Beef stock as needed (water can be used)

2 peaches cored and sliced
3 ripe pears cored and sliced
5 ripe plums, stoned and sliced
30g seedless raisins

Fry the onions in the butter till they are soft and a pale golden colour, add the minced beef and tomatoes, salt and pepper, stir well and cook for about 10 minutes. Then add enough stock to moisten, cover with a well fitting lid and cook over a low heat for about one hour, adding a little water if the meat begins to dry. Add the fruit and raisins and cook till the fruit is just soft. Do not overcook. Serve with saffron rice.

Beef as cooked in the Caribbean

100g green bacon cut in cubes
500g lean stewing beef cut into 3 × 3cm cubes
250g onions, thinly sliced
250g ripe tomatoes, peeled and cut into pieces

2 cloves of garlic sliced thinly
Pepper, salt
4 bananas cut in halves and sliced
100g smoked sausage cut into pieces

Put the green bacon into a casserole, add the beef, onions, tomatoes, garlic, salt, pepper and the bananas. Mix together, cover with a well fitting lid and cook in a slow oven for about 3 hours. Add the smoked sausage after 2½ hours.

Walnut and orange beef stew

500g stewing beef, cut into
small pieces
30g butter or oil
10 very small onions
1 large garlic clove
5dcl brown stock
1 teaspoon chopped thyme
1 tablespoon chopped
parsley

1 bay leaf
Juice of 1 orange and 1
heaped tablespoon
chopped peel
Salt, pepper
1dcl chopped walnuts
A little butter or oil to fry
the walnuts in

Put the butter into a pan, heat it and fry the meat on all sides. Add the onions and brown lightly; mash the garlic in salt and add, then add the heated stock, herbs, orange juice and peel, salt and pepper. Cover, bring to boiling point and simmer till the meat is tender, about 2 hours. Before serving, fry the walnuts in a little butter and scatter over the stew.

Spiced beef in yoghurt with walnuts

500g rump steak cut into
small squares
2 large garlic cloves
mashed with salt
3cm green ginger, chopped
very small
3 onions, thinly sliced
1 dessertspoon ground
coriander
1 teaspoon ground cumin

1 teaspoon ground
cardamom
½ teaspoon ground
turmeric
¼ teaspoon nutmeg
75g chopped walnuts
Juice of 1 lemon
3dcl of yoghurt
Sunflower oil or other
vegetable oil

Fry the garlic and ginger in a little oil for a few minutes, add the onions and fry till a light gold colour, add the spices, then the beef and the walnuts and fry together for about 5 minutes. Add the lemon juice and yoghurt. Bring to boiling point stirring all the time.

Stewed beef, marinated with lemon juice

1kg stewing beef, in one
  piece
30g butter
3 onions, thinly sliced
4 carrots cut in pieces
6dcl stock (water will do)

1 tablespoon chopped
  parsley
1 coffeespoon chopped
  thyme
1 glass red wine
30g butter
30g flour

Marinade

1 coffeespoon ground cloves
2cm crushed green ginger
1 coffeespoon ground
  cinnamon

1 coffeespoon allspice
Black pepper, salt
The juice of one lemon

Mix the ingredients of the marinade together, put the beef into a bowl and rub the marinade into it. Leave for 12 hours.

Put 30g of butter into a large pan and fry the beef in it on all sides; remove and put into a casserole. Fry the onions in the pan where the beef was fried for 5 minutes then add the carrots and fry for a few more minutes, add the stock, herbs and wine and bring to the boil. Pour the stock and vegetables over the beef and cook, covered, in a moderate oven (the liquid should just simmer) for about 3 hours. When the meat is cooked, remove and keep hot. Have the 30g of butter mixed with the 30g of flour, in small pieces and add these to the liquid. Heat, stirring till they dissolve and the sauce thickens. Put the meat back into the sauce and serve.

Veal with prunes

500g boned neck of veal, cut into pieces	2dcl white stock
25g flour	Salt, pepper
30g butter	250g prunes, soaked in water for 12 hours and then stoned
1½dcl red wine	

Dip the veal pieces in the flour, heat the butter and fry the veal in it till the pieces are golden on all sides. Then add the wine, stock and salt and pepper to taste. Mix well – the sauce should be smooth. Then add the prunes and bring to boiling point, reduce heat and simmer till the meat is tender, about an hour. At the end of cooking, the gravy should be smooth and there should only be about 3dcl. If more, reduce before serving.

Roast veal with grapes

1kg roasting veal, boned	2 dessertspoons of brandy if available
80g butter	Salt, pepper
2dcl cream	1 tablespoon sugar
The juice from 750g of white grapes (liquidize the grapes and then strain them)	1 tablespoon water
	250g seeded grapes

Tie the veal up neatly and fry on all sides in the butter, then add the cream, grape juice, brandy, salt and pepper, and mix well. Cover the pan with foil and cook in a moderate oven till the meat is done; this will take about 1½ to 2 hours. Towards the end of the cooking time put the sugar in a small pan and cook till it is a pale brown colour, then add the water and 3 tablespoons of the pan juice. Add this mixture to the meat, pouring it over the veal. Cover and cook another half hour. Put the meat in a serving dish, garnish with the seeded grapes, mix the pan juices well together and pour around the veal.

Spanish veal

1kg boneless veal in one piece
1 onion chopped small
1 coffeespoon hot paprika pepper
1 teaspoon chopped oregano

3dcl white wine
The juice of 1 orange
The juice of 1 lemon
Salt
4 tablespoons olive oil (other oil will do)

Put the veal in a neat piece into a dish. Mix the onion, paprika pepper, oregano, wine, orange and lemon juice and salt together and pour over the veal. Marinate for 6 hours. Heat the oil and add it to the veal and marinade. Roast the veal in a hot oven for an hour or longer till the meat is a nice brown colour and cooked through. Baste with the pan juices from time to time.

Veal marinated in orange and lemon juice

8 slices veal (thinly sliced and flattened)
2dcl tepid water
½ teaspoon garlic salt
¼ teaspoon freshly ground black pepper
¼ teaspoon powdered oregano (dried oregano can be powdered in an electric coffee grinder)

1 tablespoon chopped parsley
1½dcl orange juice
1½dcl lemon juice
1 dessertspoon sugar
4 tablespoon sunflower oil

Put the water with the veal slices. Mix together the garlic salt, black pepper, oregano, parsley, orange juice, lemon juice and sugar and add to the meat and water. Cover and marinate in a refrigerator for about 7 hours. Drain off the veal and fry in the oil till brown. Put the veal strips on a serving dish and heat the marinade with the oil in the pan where the veal was fried then pour over the veal and serve.

Veal with pineapple stuffing

1kg veal (this should be a
 piece from the leg,
 flattened, medium thin)
5 hard boiled eggs
2 tablespoons chopped
 chives
1 garlic clove crushed in
 salt
Pinch of nutmeg
½ coffeespoon ground
 cinnamon

200g thinly sliced
 pineapple
1dcl sour cream
50g wholewheat
 breadcrumbs
Salt, pepper
60g butter
1 teaspoon chopped
 tarragon
4dcl white stock, heated

Chop the eggs and mix together with the chives, garlic,
nutmeg, cinnamon, pineapple, sour cream and breadcrumbs; add salt and pepper to taste. Mix the butter with
the tarragon and rub over the veal. Put the filling on to
the veal and spread evenly, roll up and secure with string.
Put into a pan and roast in a moderate oven for about 2
hours. Baste frequently with the stock.

Lamb with apricots

Leg of lamb
3 medium sized cloves of
 garlic
Salt and freshly ground
 pepper

1 large onion, thinly sliced
250g dried apricots, cooked
 and made into a purée

Cut the garlic cloves into thin strips. Make little cuts into
the meat and put a piece of garlic into each. Salt the joint
and pepper it. Put the sliced onion into a baking dish and
put the joint on to a meat rack over them. Bake in a
moderate oven for about two hours. Remove excess fat
from the baking dish and then mix the pan juices and
onion with the apricot purée and pour the mixture over
the lamb. Put the meat back into the oven and cook for
another hour, basting frequently with the apricot sauce.

Lamb with damson and walnut stuffing

1 shoulder of lamb, boned
(if a cheaper cut is
preferred, use breast)
2 onions chopped small
30g butter
150g chopped walnuts
1 tablespoon chopped mint
Salt, pepper

1 tablespoon chopped
parsley
150g lamb's liver, chopped
very small
250g stoned damsons,
chopped small
1 egg

Fry the onion in butter till soft; add the walnuts, herbs, salt and pepper and the liver, simmer for about 10 minutes then add the damsons. Cook another few minutes, remove from heat and add the beaten egg. Stuff the shoulder with the mixture, secure the opening, salt and pepper the meat, and roast it in a moderate oven for about 2 hours, basting with the pan juices every 30 minutes. Use a little stock or water to baste if needed.

Syrian lamb with rice

500g lamb cut into small
cubes
1 onion, chopped small
1 clove garlic, chopped
small
4 tablespoons oil
250g rice + 6dcl of boiling
water

150g hazelnuts
Salt, pepper
1 coffeespoon cinnamon,
ground
1 tablespoon mint, chopped
small
1 tablespoon mint mixed
with 1.5dcl of yoghurt

Fry the onion and garlic in 2 tablespoons of oil till soft and golden, add the rice and stir over heat for about 3 minutes, then add 6dcl of boiling water, bring to boiling point, reduce heat and simmer till the rice is cooked and the water absorbed. Fry the nuts in 2 tablespoons of oil till light brown, remove and fry the lamb till cooked and a good brown colour. Season the lamb. Put the rice into a dish, put the nuts and lamb on top of the rice, scatter the cinnamon and mint over, mix lightly together and serve with yoghurt and chopped mint.

Turkish kortisch

1kg shoulder of lamb
1 coffeespoon salt
1 coffeespoon pepper
4 tablespoons butter (other fat will do)
4 large onions, sliced thin

8cm stick cinnamon, broken in three
5 cloves
250g prunes, soaked overnight and half cooked (they should still be firm)

Bone the lamb and rub with salt and pepper. Tie in a sausage shape. Heat the fat and fry the onions, then put the meat in and brown all over. Add a little water, enough to prevent the onions from browning too much, and the cinnamon and cloves and simmer till the meat is cooked and the liquid absorbed. Add a little water as necessary to prevent burning during the cooking process. When the meat is tender add the prunes and the liquid in which they were cooked, simmer together till the prunes are very soft.

Lamb chops marinated in lemon and oil and grilled

4 large lamb chops
1dcl lemon juice
Salt, pepper
1dcl oil
2 dessertspoons freshly cooked mint

1 teaspoon grated lemon rind
1 clove garlic mashed in salt

Put all the ingredients except the chops into a bowl and mix well together. Put the chops into a dish and pour the marinade over them. Leave for at least 3 hours. Grill, basting with the marinade till cooked through and brown.

Spiced mutton with bananas

750g mutton cut into small
  squares
1 large onion thinly sliced
1dcl of oil
1 tablespoon ground
  coriander
1 coffeespoon cayenne
  pepper

1 teaspoon turmeric
1 teaspoon ground cumin
3cm green ginger and 3
  cloves of garlic pulped
  together in water
5dcl thick yoghurt
Salt to taste
6 firm sweet bananas

Fry the onion in oil till soft and beginning to brown, add the mutton, coriander, cayenne, turmeric and cumin and fry for a few minutes, then add the garlic and ginger and fry for a few minutes longer. Add the yoghurt and continue to cook till the liquid is smooth, add salt to taste and if necessary some water or mutton stock. Simmer with a tight fitting lid till the meat is cooked, about an hour. Skin the bananas, cut into quarters and add them to the meat. Simmer together for another 20 minutes.

Skewered lamb with spiced apricot sauce

1kg lamb suitable for
  grilling
Salt, pepper
1 onion, grated
1 coffeespoon ground cumin
1 teaspoon ground
  coriander

1 coffeespoon ground
  cinnamon
1cm fresh mashed ginger
8 dried apricots
3dcl apple vinegar
15 fresh apricots, stoned
  and cut in quarters

Remove the fat from the lamb and put on one side. Cut the lamb into 2cm-squares, and salt and pepper them. Mix the onion, cumin, coriander, cinnamon and ginger with the dried apricots cut into small pieces and add the vinegar heated to boiling point. Pour over the lamb and leave to marinate for 24 hours.

Drain the lamb; put the marinade to one side. Cut the mutton fat into pieces and arrange the fresh apricot quarters, lamb cubes, and pieces of lamb fat on 12 skewers. Grill them on a hot grill until the meat is cooked and good brown colour and the fat crisp. Put the marinade through a food mill or blend in a liquidizer and serve with the lamb kebab.

Oriental lamb

1kg lamb, cut into small fatless cubes
60g unsalted butter (oil can be used)
3 large onions, chopped finely
1 coffeespoon ground cumin
1 coffeespoon ground cinnamon
1 coffeespoon ground ginger
1 coffeespoon of salt and freshly ground black pepper to taste
250g dried apricots, soaked, cooked and puréed
60g freshly ground almonds
1 teaspoon rose water
The liquid used for soaking and cooking the apricots

Heat the butter and fry the onions till soft and golden, add the lamb cubes and fry turning over till they are browned. Add the spices, salt and pepper and fry together for about 4 minutes. Add the apricot purée to the meat with the almonds, then add the rose water and stir well together. Add the cooking water from the apricots and cover with a close fitting lid. Simmer till the meat is tender and the sauce thick, about 2 hours.

Caucasian ražnjići

1kg lamb, without bone

Marinade
2dcl olive oil, or other oil
Salt, pepper
1 crushed clove

1 large clove of crushed garlic
2 tablespoons chopped parsley
1 crushed bay leaf
1 sprig of thyme

Mix all the ingredients of the marinade together. Cut the meat into squares about 4cm × 4cm. Put the meat into a bowl and pour the marinade over it, mix well into the meat and let it stand for at least 5 hours. After this time drain the meat from the marinade and arrange it on skewers. Grill on a hot grill for about ten minutes turning the skewers from time to time. Serve with chopped raw onion and salad. The marinade can be sieved, then heated and poured over the meat.

Pork cooked with fruits

500g pork (spare-rib is good)
250g stewing beef, cut up into chunks
30g butter
4 large tomatoes, skinned and chopped
1 large onion, chopped small
1 chilli

4 large bay leaves
½ small coffeespoon cayenne pepper
2 heaped tablespoons rice (brown rice is best)
3 large slices pineapple, cut into pieces
3 ripe bananas, sliced
Salt

Fry the pork and beef in the butter till they are pale brown, then put into a pan with the tomatoes, onions, chilli, bay leaves and cayenne pepper. Simmer for a few minutes, then add the rice and just enough water to cover the ingredients. Add salt and simmer till the stew thickens. Add the fruit and continue to simmer for approximately an hour.

Pork with gooseberry stuffing

1kg loin of pork, boned
250g gooseberries
50g breadcrumbs
1 tablespoon chopped herbs
    (sage, lemon balm, mint)

20g brown sugar
1 egg
3dcl stock or water
Salt, pepper

Mash half the gooseberries with the breadcrumbs, herbs and half the sugar. Beat the egg and mix well with the gooseberries and crumbs. Spread the mixture over the pork and roll up and tie neatly. Put the remaining gooseberries with the rest of the sugar, add a little water and cook till they are soft, then purée them. Salt the pork roll and roast it in a moderate oven for about 2 hours. When the pork is cooked put on to a serving dish and keep hot. Mix the meat juices with the gooseberry purée and water or stock and heat to boiling point. Serve with the pork roll as a sauce.

Roast orange pork

2kg leg of pork
1 tablespoon chopped fresh
    sage
Salt, pepper
1 clove garlic, mashed with
    salt

Grated rind of 1 orange
1 tablespoon redcurrant
    jelly
3 large ripe oranges and
    1dcl orange juice + 1dcl
    water or stock

Mix the sage with salt, pepper and garlic and rub into the pork. Bake in a moderate oven for 2 hours, then sprinkle the grated orange over the pork, spread the redcurrant jelly on the skin and pour over it the orange juice diluted with an equal quantity of water or stock. Cook for another 30 minutes or till the pork is done, basting frequently. Clean the skins of the remaining oranges and cut them into thick slices, leaving the skin on. Put these around and on the pork and cook for another 15 minutes or till the orange segments are hot.

Pork chops, sweet potatoes and apples

4 pork chops
500g parboiled sweet
potatoes (parsnips can be
used instead)

8 small apples, cored and
filled with seeded raisins

Stuffing
150g dry breadcrumbs
1dcl melted butter
Salt, pepper
1 coffeespoon each chopped
thyme, sage, lemon balm,
mixed together (or other
herbs as available)

1 tablespoon chopped onion
(or spring onions or
chives if preferred)
1 teaspoon chopped parsley
1 egg yolk

Put the chops on to a baking dish. Mix all the ingredients
for the stuffing and spread over the surface of each chop.
Put the sweet potatoes around them in the dish, and also
the apples. Bake in a hot oven for about an hour, basting
from time to time with water.

Baked pork with prunes

1kg roasting pork
Salt, pepper
2dcl white wine (or you can
substitute whey)
500g prunes

30g flour
30g butter
2dcl sour cream or thick
yoghurt

Rub salt and pepper into the pork and put it to roast in a
moderate oven. Put the wine and prunes together in a pan
and bring to the boil. Baste the meat with the warmed
wine three times in the first hour of cooking, then remove
the pork from the roasting dish. Put the prunes and a
tablespoon of wine into the dish and put the pork on top.
Cook the meat in the oven till it is done (about 45 minutes
more) then remove to a serving dish and keep warm.

Mix the butter and flour together. Put the wine and the

juices from the meat and the prunes into a pan; bring to the boil. Add the cream and heat to simmering point then add the butter and flour mixture in little pieces. Stir over the heat till the sauce thickens. Serve with the prunes in the same dish as the meat and the sauce in a separate dish.

Lacquered pork chops

4 pork chops
The juice of one large
   lemon
½ coffeespoon paprika
   pepper
¼ coffeespoon grated
   nutmeg

½ coffeespoon ground
   cinnamon
50g butter, melted
Salt

Sauce
250g ripe plums
1dcl lemon juice
1dcl honey
2cm green ginger, pounded
   and mixed with 3
   tablespoons water (this
   can be done best in a
   blender)

Black pepper
A pinch of cayenne pepper

Marinate the pork chops for at least 6 hours in the lemon juice, paprika pepper, nutmeg and cinnamon.

To make the sauce, cook the plums in the lemon juice and honey till the mixture has the consistency of jam. Add the ginger infusion, black pepper and cayenne pepper.

Remove the chops from the marinade and salt them. Grill them, basting them with the melted butter. When they are cooked rub half the plum sauce over one side of each chop and grill that side under a very hot grill till glazed. Then turn the chops over, cover the other sides with the remaining sauce and grill till glazed. Serve at once.

Pancakes stuffed with pork and banana

8 large pancakes
1 tablespoon chopped onion
30g butter
1 large tomato chopped small
500g pork, chopped small

Salt, pepper
1 egg
1 large banana
The grated rind of 1 orange

Sauce
3dcl tomato juice
1 clove garlic, mashed with salt

1 tablespoon chopped parsley
1 bay leaf, broken in pieces
Salt and pepper

Make the sauce first. Put the tomato juice in a pan with the garlic, pepper and salt, parsley and bay leaf and simmer till the juice is reduced by one-third. Strain.

Fry the onion in butter till soft, add the tomato and cook for five minutes, then add the meat, salt and pepper and the sauce and bring to the boil. Reduce heat and simmer for about 30 minutes. Beat the egg and stir into the meat, then add the banana, sliced into small strips, and the grated orange peel. Simmer for another 10 minutes, stirring gently. Fill the pancakes and roll up. Put in a shallow dish, put any remaining meat on top of the pancakes, reheat if necessary and serve with the sauce.

Pork chops with fruit stuffing

4 pork chops (at least 3cm thick)
Salt, pepper

Flour
Pork fat for frying
Stuffing (see below)

Cut the chops halfway through sideways to the bone. Stuff the cavity and fasten with toothpicks or similar wooden skewers. Season with salt and pepper, dip in flour and fry quickly in hot fat on both sides to a golden brown colour. Then place the chops on a rack in a baking dish, cover closely with foil or a lid and roast for about 45 minutes.

Use one of the following stuffings:

Apple stuffing I

Use the recipe on page 54, adding 2dcl of raw grated apple.

Apple stuffing II

100g chopped salt pork	1 tablespoon chopped
100g chopped onion	parsley
5 apples, cored and cut into	50g dry breadcrumbs
small pieces	Salt, pepper
2 tablespoons brown sugar	Pork fat

Fry the salt pork in the fat till it is crisp. Remove and fry the onions in the same fat till they are softened, remove from the fat and put the apples into the pan. Add sugar to taste and cook over a low heat till they are soft; add the salt, pepper, parsley and breadcrumbs and the pork and onions, and the stuffing is ready to use.

Prune stuffing

Use the previous recipe, substituting soaked stoned prunes for the apples.

Pork chops in fruit aspic

4 cooked pork chops	Pickled gherkins for
3dcl pineapple juice	garnishing
15g gelatine (about half an	Salt, pepper
envelope of powdered	
gelatine)	

Heat the pineapple juice and dissolve the gelatine in it. Put into the refrigerator till the pineapple begins to set, then dip each chop in the jelly. Put them in a serving dish, pour the remaining jelly over them, garnish with sliced gherkins. Put into the refrigerator to set.

Belly of pork with pears

2kg belly of pork
200g onions, thinly sliced
1 sprig sage
2 tablespoons cider vinegar
Pepper, salt

500g pears (these can be cooking pears, cored and cut into quarters. You can peel them, but this will reduce the taste)
1 coffeespoon mustard powder

Cut the pork into about 10 pieces and put into a pan. Add enough hot water just to cover the pork, add the onions, sage, salt and cider vinegar. Bring to the boil and then reduce heat and simmer till the meat is tender, about 1 hour. Remove the meat and keep hot. Strain the liquid, reheat and poach the pears in it till just cooked. Arrange the pears round the pork, and serve the liquid, seasoned with mustard and pepper, in a separate dish.

Galloping horses from Thailand

750g minced lean pork
1 tablespoon chopped garlic
125g chopped peanuts
1 coffeespoon ground coriander
1 coffeespoon (or less if preferred) ground red chilli peppers

1 coffeespoon mashed anchovies
Salt to taste
8 large oranges with the skins well washed
½dcl sunflower oil

Heat the oil and fry the garlic till it begins to brown. Add the pork, peanuts, coriander, chilli peppers, anchovy paste and a little salt (do not add too much), and cook on a low heat, stirring gently, for about 15 minutes. Cut the oranges, unpeeled, into quarters, leaving the skins connected at the bottom. Each orange will then be a cup. Remove the pips and press the inside fruit so that there will be room to put in the pork and peanut stuffing. Fill the insides of the oranges with the pork mixture. Put the oranges on to a baking dish and bake for about 15 minutes in a moderately hot oven.

Spiced pineapple pork

2kg roasting pork
2 teaspoons freshly ground coriander
1 coffeespoon salt
1 teaspoon freshly ground black pepper
1 large clove garlic, mashed in salt

2 tablespoons soy sauce
1 tablespoon cider vinegar
1 large ripe fresh pineapple, skinned, cored and sliced

Mix the coriander, salt, pepper and garlic together, rub over the meat. Put the meat into a roasting pan, cover with foil and roast for two hours in a moderate oven. Mix the soy sauce with the vinegar and baste the meat with it; cook for another half hour, uncovered, basting frequently. When cooked, put the meat into a serving dish, garnish with pineapple slices and serve with the pan juices.

Pork chops with golden plums

8 pork chops
1 large onion, chopped small
Sunflower oil

250g golden plums
1 glass white wine
½ glass wine vinegar
½ glass white stock

Fry the onion in a little oil till soft and golden. Sauté the chops in oil and when they are half cooked add the onion and cook over a low heat till the meat is done. Have the plums ready stoned and cooked in a small quantity of water till soft, but not mushy. Dilute the pan juices with a small glass of white wine and the wine vinegar and stock. Reheat to boiling point. Serve the chops on a round plate in a circle with the plums in the middle and the sauce poured over the meat.

Tartlets filled with pork and cranberries

500g cooked boneless pork,
  cut into small pieces
200g onions, chopped small
30g butter
Salt, pepper

1 teaspoon chopped lemon
  balm
1 tablespoon chopped
  parsley
2dcl cranberry purée

Pastry
200g butter
350g flour
Salt

1 egg yolk
Cold water as needed

Make the pastry first. Mix the butter into the flour with a little salt. Mix in the beaten egg yolk and enough cold water to make a pliable dough. Leave to rest for about 30 minutes.

Cook the onions in the butter till soft. Mix with the chopped pork, salt, pepper, lemon balm, parsley, and cranberry purée. Line flan cases with pastry, fill with the mixture, cover with a layer of pastry, make a small hole in the top of each case to allow steam to escape, and bake in a hot oven for about 30 minutes, or till a good brown colour.

Pork fruit sandwiches

8 thin pork chops
16 prunes, soaked, stoned
  and cut into pieces
2 large apples, cut into
  small pieces
The grated peel of 1 lemon

1 beaten egg
Dry breadcrumbs as needed
  (wheatgerm makes a
  good substitute)
Salt and pepper
Pork fat

Flatten the pork chops with a meat hammer till they are very thin. Mix the prunes and apple together, add the lemon rind and pepper and spread over 4 of the chops. Cover with the other chops. Tie a cotton thread across each one to secure it. Dip each sandwich into beaten egg and then into breadcrumbs, sprinkle with salt and fry in pork fat until they are a nice brown colour. Remove the cotton.

Lemon pork chops

4 pork chops
The juice of 3 lemons
1 clove garlic, mashed in salt
1 teaspoon allspice

Pinch each of nutmeg, cinnamon and ground clove
Freshly ground black pepper, salt

Make a marinade of the lemon juice, garlic and spices and rub into the pork. Put in a cool place for about 12 hours, then salt and pepper the chops and grill them.

Pork, liver and ham rolls

500g lean pork
250g pigs' liver
100g ham
1 teaspoon chopped fresh sage
1 teaspoon lemon balm
1 dessertspoon chopped chives

1½dcl fresh breadcrumbs
Salt, pepper, oil as needed
2 egg yolks
2 onions, thinly sliced
500g small apples, cored and sliced

Cut the pork into thin slices and flatten them – they should end up about 6cm × 6cm. Chop the liver and ham small and mix with the herbs, breadcrumbs, salt and pepper. Heat a little oil in a pan and cook this mixture for a few minutes, then remove from the heat and add the egg yolks, well beaten. Spread this mixture on the pork slices and roll up, tying with cotton to secure well. Heat some oil in a large pan and fry the rolls, browning them on all sides, Add the onions and the apples. Cook slowly till the meat, onions and apples are cooked and a good brown colour. Add a little stock or water if necessary and serve with the pan juices.

Pork pie with apple

500g pork
Salt, pepper
1 teaspoon chopped sage
2 onions

300g potatoes
3 large apples
2dcl stock
20g pork fat (pork dripping)

Cut the pork into small pieces, sprinkle with salt, pepper and sage and mix well together. Cut the onions in thin slices, cut the potatoes in thin slices, and core and peel the apples and slice them. Grease a pie dish and put the ingredients into it in layers, ending with a layer of potatoes. Pour over the stock and dot the pork fat over the top. Bake in a moderately hot oven, covered with foil. Cook for 2 hours. Half an hour before it is cooked, remove the foil and let the top brown.

Loin of pork with prunes

1½kg pork loin
250g soaked prunes, stoned

1 garlic clove crushed in
salt

Have the pork loin boned. Stuff it with the prunes, roll it up, rub with the crushed garlic and put in a roasting dish. Roast in a hot oven for about 1½ hours.

Baked ham with fruit juice

1 ham joint

Basting sauce
The juice of 2 large oranges
2dcl pineapple juice

1dcl honey

Put the ham with the fat side upwards in an oven dish and bake in a slow oven for 25 minutes per half kilo.

Make the basting sauce by mixing together the juices and honey. 45 minutes before the ham is cooked, remove it

on a wicker tray and plunge into a big pan of boiling water (removing the tray) and poach for about 20 minutes. As the sausages rise to the surface of the water prick them with a needle to let the air out. Remove the sausages from the water and drain on the wicker tray. Do not cool too quickly or the sausages will become dry.

Before grilling or frying, prick the sausages with a fork on both sides and then cook on a moderate heat.

To make an English version of the black pudding add 500g of cooked rice or pearl barley to the mixture before stuffing the intestine.

Braised ox tongue

1 fresh ox tongue
1 sliced onion
2 bay leaves
5 cloves
Salt, pepper
50g bacon fat
3 carrots, chopped small
2 onions, chopped small
1 turnip, chopped small
4 celery stalks, chopped small
Flour
1 large sprig of parsley, sprig of thyme and sage
The juice of 1 lemon

Wash the tongue well and put into a pan with enough hot water to cover it. Add the onion, bay leaves, cloves, salt and pepper and bring to the boil, then reduce the heat and simmer for about 2 hours. Remove the tongue from the pan, trim it and remove the coarse skin.

Put the bacon fat into a pan, add the vegetables and fry till they begin to brown. Remove them from the pan. Flour the tongue all over and fry on all sides in the fat, then put the vegetables back with the tongue, add 1 litre of stock from the first cooking of the tongue, and the herbs. Simmer for about one hour, then add the lemon juice and cook for half an hour simmering gently. When the tongue is cooked, remove and keep hot. Reduce the pan juices till you have just enough to pour around the tongue. Remove the herb sprigs before serving.

Spanish tongue

6 lambs' tongues
1 onion
1 bay leaf
Mixed herbs (oregano,
    parsley, lemon balm)
1 carrot
Salt and pepper

1 lemon cut in thin slices
2dcl brown sugar
3dcl seedless raisins
8 cloves
1½dcl cider vinegar
3dcl stock from cooking the
    tongues

Put the tongues into a pan with the onion, bay leaf, mixed herbs, carrot and some freshly ground pepper and salt. Cover with cold water, bring to the boil and simmer till tender.

Put the lemon slices, sugar, raisins, cloves, vinegar and stock into a pan, bring to the boil and simmer for about an hour. Put the cooked tongues on to a serving dish and pour the sauce over them.

This sauce can be served with any kind of tongue.

Fresh tongue with grapes and almonds

1 calf's tongue, cooked,
    skinned and sliced in
    thick slices
25g butter
75g blanched almonds,
    shredded
200g white grapes (seeded
    if required)

Salt, pepper
The juice of ½ lemon
1 dessertspoon flour
1 dessertspoon butter
3dcl white stock
1 glass dry sherry

Heat the butter and fry the almonds till they are pale brown. Add the grapes, salt, pepper and lemon juice. Have ready a sauce made from the flour, butter and stock, add it to the grapes and almonds, pour in the sherry and simmer for 5 minutes. Pour the sauce over the tongue, reheat if necessary and serve.

Roast beef heart with walnut stuffing

1 beef heart
50g butter
1 onion, chopped small
100g chopped walnuts
1 egg
60g breadcrumbs

Apple juice to moisten the stuffing (blackcurrant or redcurrant juice can also be used)
Salt, pepper

For cooking the heart
3dcl apple juice
1dcl oil

Melt the butter and fry the chopped onion in it till pale golden. Add the nuts and fry for a few minutes, then add the egg, well beaten, breadcrumbs and enough apple juice to moisten the stuffing. Season.

Clean the heart, fill it with the stuffing and cover the opening with foil. Heat the oil in a roasting pan, put the heart into it and roast in a moderately hot oven, basting with the heated apple juice every 15 minutes. Cook for 2 hours. Serve with the pan juices and, if liked, apple sauce or redcurrant jelly.

Prunes stuffed with sausagemeat

250g large prunes
250g sausagemeat
1 teaspoon lemon balm
1 teaspoon chopped parsley
½ teaspoon fresh chopped sage

4 spring onions, chopped small (including the green part)
Salt, pepper

Cook the prunes in water till they are soft (do not overcook). Mix the sausagemeat, herbs, onion and salt and pepper together. Stone the prunes and stuff with the sausagemeat mixture. Bake in a hot oven for about 30 minutes.

Stewed oxtail with lemon

1 oxtail cut into 4cm
   lengths
Flour to coat the oxtail
   pieces
60g fat bacon cut into small
   cubes
2 carrots

2 onions
A sprig each of thyme,
   sage, parsley, tarragon
Salt, pepper
6dcl brown stock (if not
   available use water)
The juice of 1 lemon

Melt the bacon cubes in a pan and fry the oxtail pieces coated in flour in the fat. Add the carrots and onions, cut into small pieces, the herbs, salt and pepper. Have the stock heated to boiling point and add to the oxtail. Simmer till the oxtail is done (about 2½ to 3 hours) then add the lemon juice and serve.

POULTRY AND GAME

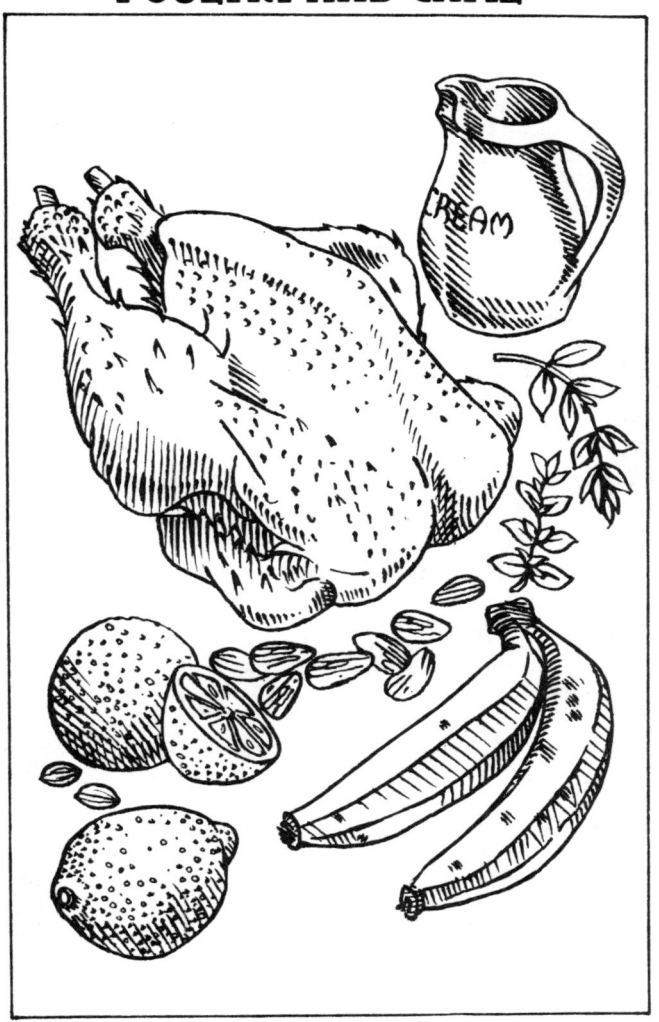

Chicken and almond mousse

3 egg yolks
½ coffeespoon paprika
1 coffeespoon salt
3dcl chicken stock
1 tablespoon fresh chopped
 tarragon
1 tablespoon gelatine
 soaked in 1 tablespoon
 lemon juice

1 cooked chicken breast,
 chopped very small
120g blanched almonds,
 chopped very finely or
 ground
1dcl cream

Put the egg yolks into a bowl and beat a little. Add the salt
and paprika pepper, then beat in the stock, little by little,
then add the tarragon. Put the bowl over a pan of boiling
water and cook, stirring all the time, till the mixture
thickens. Add the gelatine and stir till it dissolves. Mix
the chicken and almonds together and combine with the
mixture in the bowl. Put to cool. When the mixture begins
to set, beat the cream and fold it into the mousse. Put into
a serving bowl and chill.

Peach chicken

1 roasting chicken
 weighing approx 1½kg
3 onions, sliced thin
60g butter
4 ripe peaches
¼ coffeespoon grated
 nutmeg
Rind of ½ lemon

Salt, pepper
3dcl chicken stock
Juice of 1 lemon
2dcl sour cream
1 dessertspoon chopped
 lemon balm (if available)

Cut the chicken into serving pieces. Fry the onions in the
butter till they are a light golden colour, then add the
peaches, stoned and cut into quarters. Fry for a few
minutes. Remove the onions and peaches with a slotted
spoon. Fry the chicken in the pan where the onions were
fried till the pieces are a light golden brown on all sides.

Put into a casserole with the onions and peaches, the nutmeg, lemon rind, salt, pepper and stock. Cover the dish and simmer in the oven for about an hour. When the chicken is cooked, remove from the casserole and pour the juices into a pan. Return the chicken to the casserole and keep hot. Bring the pan juices to the boil, add the lemon juice and reheat to boiling point, then add the sour cream and reheat again to boiling point. Pour the sauce over the chicken and serve scattered with chopped lemon balm.

Lemon chicken

1 roasting chicken (approx 1½kg)
100g butter
Salt, pepper

The juice of 2 lemons plus an equal quantity of hot water

Fry the chicken in hot butter till light brown on all sides. Put into a fireproof dish. Mix the hot water and lemon juice, add salt and pepper and pour over the chicken. Cook in a moderately hot oven for about an hour, basting with the lemon liquid every 15 minutes. Serve with the pan juices.

Chicken cooked with orange juice and onions

1 chicken (about 1½kg)
400g onions, sliced thinly
40g butter

Salt, pepper
4dcl orange juice

Cook the sliced onions in the butter till soft but not brown. Put them into an oven dish large enough to take the chicken and place the chicken on top. Add salt and pepper to the orange juice and pour over the chicken. Cook in a moderately hot oven for about 1 hour, basting every 15 minutes. Serve the chicken in the dish it was cooked in, with the orange onion sauce.

Chicken livers cooked with orange

8 chicken livers
1 onion chopped small
1 large clove garlic, mashed
   with salt
30g butter
2dcl orange juice
Salt, pepper

1 heaped tablespoon
   chopped parsley
1 large orange (the peel
   grated and the flesh
   sliced across in medium
   thick slices)

Fry the onion and mashed garlic in the butter till soft. Add the liver and fry for about 5 minutes till brown on all sides. Pour the orange juice over and stir. Add salt and pepper to taste, and the chopped parsley. Put the orange slices and peel in the pan and heat together for about 5 minutes on a low heat. Serve in the pan it was cooked in.

Chicken with walnut sauce

1 chicken weighing about
   1½kg + the giblets
1 large carrot, chopped
1 large onion, sliced
2 large cloves garlic,
   crushed
Salt, freshly ground black
   pepper
1 large sprig oregano

Sauce
100g white breadcrumbs
Chicken stock as needed
450g chopped walnuts
1 dessertspoon fresh
   chopped oregano (if
   dried, use 1 teaspoon)
2 large cloves garlic
1 teaspoon paprika pepper
Salt and pepper

Put the chicken in a pan and cover with hot water. Add the carrot, onion, crushed garlic, chicken giblets, salt and pepper and sprig of oregano. Poach the chicken for about 1 hour, then cool it in the cooking water. When it is cold, drain off the stock and put to one side. Remove the chicken meat carefully from the bones.

To make the sauce, soak the breadcrumbs in a little chicken stock. When they have absorbed the liquid, drain to remove any excess. Put the breadcrumbs and walnuts through a mincing machine twice, or through a mouli-grater. Add the oregano to the mixture. Crush 2 cloves of garlic with the paprika, add to the walnut mixture and add salt and pepper to taste. Boil the chicken stock and reduce by half. Cool, then add the stock to the walnut mixture, beating gently till the sauce has the consistency of double cream. Arrange the chicken pieces on a serving dish, pour the sauce over it and garnish with chopped parsley.

Chicken with banana

1 chicken (about 1½kg)
Salt, pepper
1dcl melted butter
1dcl madeira, if available
1dcl sour cream (increase this to 2dcl if you are not using madeira)
4 ripe bananas
Oil for frying

Batter
250g flour
1 egg
2dcl milk
Salt

Salt and pepper the chicken, put into a roasting pan and pour the melted butter over it. Roast in a hot oven for about 1 hour. When the chicken is cooked, remove and cut into serving pieces and keep hot in a heated dish.

Put the madeira into the pan juices and cook together, stirring, for about 5 minutes. Then add the sour cream, mix well and bring to the boil. Remove from the heat and keep warm.

Have the batter ready. Mix the flour with the beaten egg. Then add the milk (enough to make the batter a little thicker than pancake batter), add salt and beat till the batter is smooth.

Skin the bananas and cut them into pieces (about 6 pieces to a banana). Heat the oil, dip the banana pieces in the batter and deep fry till crisp and golden brown. Put the banana pieces with the chicken and serve the sauce separately.

Chicken stuffed with prunes, orange and herbs

1 roasting chicken
100g butter
1 teaspoon oregano
1 teaspoon lemon balm
A pinch each of basil and
    thyme
Salt

150g cooked brown rice
1 large orange, peeled and
    chopped small (if liked,
    the peel can be chopped
    small and added)
100g cooked prunes, stoned
    and chopped small

Mix the butter with the herbs and rub into the skin of the chicken. Salt the chicken. Mix the rice with the orange and prunes, add a little salt if liked, and stuff the chicken with the mixture. Roast in a moderately hot oven.

Chicken cooked with tarragon and served with grapes

1 chicken (about 1½kg in
    weight)
1 tablespoon chopped
    tarragon
50g butter
250g grapes

Juice of ½ lemon
3dcl white stock
1dcl sour cream (or fresh
    cream with a little lemon
    juice added)
Salt, pepper

Mix the tarragon and butter together and rub into the chicken, saving a small piece of the tarragon butter to put in the cavity. Salt and pepper the chicken and put into a roasting pan. Roast for about 1 hour.

Seed the grapes if necessary and mix them with the lemon juice. Cut the roasted chicken into serving pieces and keep hot. Pour the stock into the roasting pan and scrape round the dish to remove the pan juices. Put into a small pan and boil, reducing the liquid by half. Add the sour cream, reheat, then add the grapes and serve the sauce poured over the chicken.

Chicken with orange and lemon sauce

1 roasting chicken

Basting sauce

3dcl stock	1dcl lemon juice
6dcl orange juice	Salt as needed

Mix the ingredients for the basting sauce together. Put the chicken into a baking dish and pour about half the sauce over it. Put into a moderately hot oven, and as the chicken cooks, baste with the remaining sauce.

Duck with orange sauce

1 duck	1 small veal bone
30g butter	1 gill white wine
2 tablespoons brandy	1 gill meat stock
3 large carrots	Salt, pepper
1 small bay leaf	3 oranges
3 sprigs parsley	1 tablespoon sugar
2 sprigs thyme	

Clean and truss the duck. Heat the butter and brown the duck all over in it, then remove from the heat, pour the brandy over the duck and set it alight.

Cut the carrots into pieces and put them with the bay leaf, parsley, thyme and veal bone around the duck in an oven dish. Pour the wine and stock over the duck and season with salt and pepper. Cover the oven dish and put into a medium hot oven to cook for one hour. Strain the sauce in which the duck was cooked and add the juice of one orange and some grated rind. Boil this sauce for 5 minutes. Cook the sugar to make caramel and add it to the sauce, then boil a few more minutes. Skin and slice the two remaining oranges and put them into boiling water for 2 minutes. Put the duck into a serving dish, surround with slices of orange, pour sauce over and serve.

Duck with cherries

1 duck
50g butter
Salt, pepper

500g cherries (these should
be sweet black cherries)
3dcl red wine

Cover the duck with the butter, salt and pepper it and roast in a hot oven. Baste it from time to time with a little boiling water to begin with, then with the pan juices. Cook the cherries by simmering them in the red wine; stone them. Put the cooked duck on a serving dish, mix the cherries and the wine they were cooked in with the pan juices. Put the cherries around the duck and pour the pan juices over it. If preferred the sauce can be served separately.

Duck with pineapple sauce

1 duck, cut into serving
pieces
30g butter
1 ripe pineapple, skinned
and cut into slices

1 glass white wine
1 clove garlic, crushed in
salt
Salt, pepper

Orange pineapple sauce
15g cornflour
The juice and grated rind
from 1 orange
Juices from the duck, plus,
if necessary, some water
to make up 3dcl of liquid

Pineapple (the remaining
half, each slice cut into
quarters)
100g seedless raisins

Soften the butter and rub into the duck pieces, then put them into a roasting pan. Crush half the pineapple slices, or put them into a blender, with the wine. Put the resulting purée with the duck and add the garlic and pepper. Cook in a moderately hot oven for about an hour, basting every 15 minutes.

While the duck is cooking mix the cornflour with the

orange juice. Heat the pan juices and stir in the cornflour and orange. Simmer till the sauce thickens, then add the remaining pineapple, the raisins and the grated orange rind. Reheat and serve.

Duck with apples

1 duck
80g butter
Salt, pepper

6dcl cider
2dcl sour cream
1kg apples

Rub the duck with 50g of butter and salt and pepper. Put into an oven dish and roast in a hot oven for about an hour. Remove the duck from the oven dish and put on a serving dish and keep hot. Pour the cider into the oven dish and boil on top of the stove, scraping the sides of the dish to remove the juices. Boil till the cider and juices are well blended, then add the sour cream and simmer for about 15 minutes. Core the apples and quarter them. Fry in the remaining 30g of butter till soft, adding a little cider if necessary. Serve the apples round the duck and the sauce separately.

Roast goose with prune and apple stuffing

1 roasting goose
1kg apples
250g prunes, soaked and
    stoned
1 tablespoon demerara
    sugar

Peel of ½ a lemon
50g butter
Salt, pepper

Core the apples and cut them into pieces; stone the prunes and cut them into pieces. Mix together and add the sugar and lemon peel. Put this stuffing into the goose, rub the skin with butter, salt and pepper it and roast in a moderately hot oven till done (25 minutes to the half kilogram).

Goose with apple and ham stuffing and chestnut side dish

1 goose

Stuffing

100g dried breadcrumbs
Milk or stock
1 goose liver
70g ham, chopped very small
2 onions, chopped small
2 tablespoons chopped parsley

1 garlic clove crushed in salt
1 egg
Salt and pepper
3 large eating apples, cored and cut into small pieces, or grated

Soak the breadcrumbs in the milk or stock, then drain so that they are not too wet. Chop the goose liver and mix with the ham, breadcrumbs, onion, parsley, garlic and beaten egg. Add salt and pepper to taste, then the chopped apple. Mix well together and stuff the goose. Sew up, or secure well.

Make the following mixture

1 onion, chopped small
100g goose fat or oil
1 large carrot, thinly sliced

2 tablespoons chopped parsley
1 teaspoon chopped thyme
1dcl stock

Fry the onion in 60g of the goose fat, add the carrot, parsley, thyme and 1dcl of stock. Put the mixture into a heavy roasting pan and put the goose on top, first rubbing the remaining goose fat or oil into the skin. Roast in a moderately hot oven till the bird is tender and the skin is a golden brown colour, about 2 hours.

The chestnut side dish

150g ham
80g butter

60 shelled chestnuts
8dcl stock

Fry the ham in 60g of the butter till it turns a pale brown

80

colour. Add the chestnuts and the remaining stock and simmer together till the chestnuts are tender, about 30 minutes. Remove any excess stock and add the remaining butter to the chestnuts.

Serve the goose with the pan juices sieved and poured over it and the chestnuts served separately.

Roast goose with apple stuffing

1 small goose
300g eating apples
Salt, pepper

1 tablespoon chopped
   oregano
Brown sugar as needed

Core the apples and put some brown sugar inside each. Put these inside the bird, rub the outside of the bird with salt, pepper and oregano. Bake in a moderately hot oven for about 40 minutes per kilogram.

Turkey with orange juice and spices

500g turkey breast
Flour
50g butter
3dcl orange juice
Salt, pepper
1 red pepper, seeded and
   chopped into dice

100g sultanas
1 coffeespoon chilli pepper
1 coffeespoon dried ginger,
   or 2cm fresh ginger
1 tablespoon sugar
1 tablespoon cider vinegar

Cut the turkey breast into cubes, dredge them in flour and sauté them in butter. When the pieces are golden brown, remove them and put into a pan. Pour the orange juice into the pan the turkey was cooked in and mix with the pan juices; season with salt and pepper and pour over the turkey. Add the sultanas, red pepper, chilli pepper, ginger (if green ginger is used, mash it with a little of the orange juice), sugar and vinegar. Simmer together for 45 minutes, if necessary adding more orange juice.

This dish should be cooked and reheated as it improves with keeping. It is a good dish for freezing.

Turkey with cherries

1kg turkey breast
50g butter
1kg sweet cherries
3dcl water

1 tablespoon white wine
vinegar
Salt, pepper

Cut the turkey breast into slices and fry in the butter. Cook the cherries in the water mixed with the vinegar. When they are just soft, strain and remove the stones. Put the cherries and the turkey in a casserole, mix the cherry water with the pan juices from frying the turkey and pour over. Bring to the boil, reduce heat, add salt and pepper to taste and simmer till the turkey is tender. This will take about 45 minutes.

Quail with cherries

4 quails
100g butter

500g cherries, stoned

Sauté the quails in the butter till they are almost cooked. Add the cherries, cover with a well fitting lid and cook in a slow oven till the cherries are soft. Do not add any liquid or sugar in the cooking.

Quail with grapes

4 quails, cleaned and
plucked
4 large vine leaves
4 slices fat bacon

30g butter
500g grapes, seeded
½ wine glass brandy
1 wine glass stock

Wrap each quail in a vine leaf, then in a slice of bacon and tie up. Heat the butter in a pan and sauté the quails for about 15 minutes. Remove them to a shallow earthenware casserole and add the grapes. Pour over them the fat from the pan. Cook in a hot oven for 15 minutes. Remove the quails and grapes and keep warm. Dilute the juices in the casserole with the brandy and stock, bring to the boil, pour over the quails and serve.

Stewed rabbit with orange and grapefruit

1 rabbit, cut into serving
   pieces, marinated
   overnight in yoghurt,
   salt and pepper
100g fat green bacon or salt
   pork
2 large onions, thinly sliced
Juice of 1 orange
1 grapefruit
1 clove garlic mashed in
   salt

1 dessertspoon mixed
   chopped herbs (sage,
   thyme, lemon balm,
   parsley)
1 tablespoon chopped
   chives
Stock or water
100g raisins

Put the bacon in a pan and heat till the fat begins to run. Add the pieces of rabbit and fry till they are a pale brown. Then add the onion slices and fry till pale golden. Now add the orange juice, grapefruit flesh (pulped), garlic, herbs, and stock, heated to boiling point (enough just to cover the rabbit). Bring to the boil and simmer, covered with a tight fitting lid, till the rabbit is tender, about 2 hours. Add the raisins after about 1 hour. Serve with boiled brown rice.

Prunes with rabbit

1 rabbit
3dcl red wine
1 large bay leaf, crushed
1 large sprig thyme
2 tablespoons red wine
   vinegar

3 crushed peppercorns
Flour
50g butter
Salt, pepper
500g prunes, soaked and
   stoned

Marinate the rabbit in the wine, herbs and vinegar and peppercorns for about 12 hours. Pour the marinade off the rabbit and reserve it. Drain the rabbit on absorbent paper, then dip in flour and fry in the butter on all sides till golden brown. Put into a pan and add the marinade (strained) to cover the rabbit. Season with salt and pepper, add the prunes, cover with a well fitting lid and simmer on a low heat till the rabbit is tender, about 1½ hours.

Spiced rabbit

1 rabbit, cut into serving
    pieces
3 onions
100g butter

3dcl yoghurt
1dcl lemon juice
4 eating apples
30g large raisins

Spice mixture
1 teaspoon ground cumin
1 dessertspoon ground
    coriander
½ teaspoon turmeric
3 cloves garlic, chopped
    small
3cm piece of green ginger,
    peeled and chopped
1 teaspoon ground
    cardamom seeds
1 coffeespoon ground
    cinnamon

½ coffeespoon ground
    cloves
Salt, pepper, cayenne
    pepper if liked
(If preferred, you can use 1
    level tablespoon of curry
    powder and 1 of garam
    masala instead of this
    spice mixture)

Slice the onions thinly and fry them in the butter till soft and a golden colour. Then add the mixture of spices, garlic and ginger and fry for about 4 minutes. Add the rabbit pieces, fry for about 4 minutes, turning them to brown on all sides. Add the yoghurt and simmer, stirring, till well blended. Then add the lemon juice and simmer with a tightly fitting lid for about 1 hour. Core the apples and cut into slices, add to the stew with the raisins and simmer for another hour. Serve with rice.

VEGETARIAN DISHES

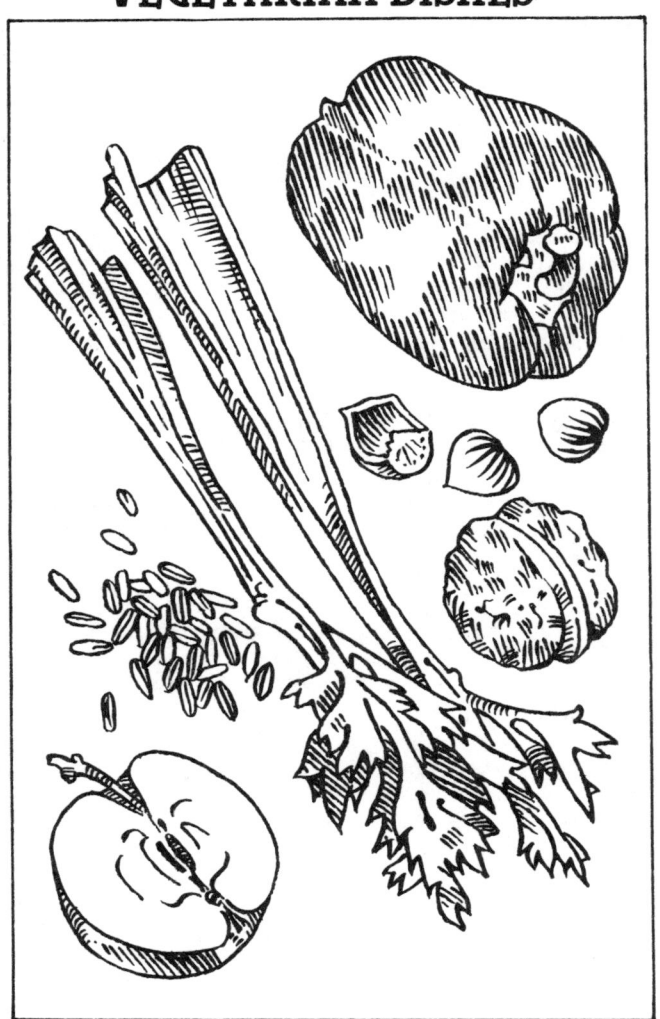

Nut celery loaf

75g chopped celery
1 onion, chopped small
75g chopped nuts
(hazelnuts, walnuts, etc.)
2dcl tomato juice
1 tablespoon melted butter
Garlic salt to taste (about 1 teaspoon)
1 teaspoon salt
100g dry brown breadcrumbs (put 2 dessertspoonfuls to one side for the topping)

1 egg
1 tablespoon grated Parmesan cheese or other hard cheese
2 tablespoons oil
2 tablespoons chopped parsley

Mix the celery, onion and nuts together, add the tomato juice, butter, garlic, salt and breadcrumbs. Beat the egg and add it; then add the Parmesan. Mix everything well together with the oil. Grease a baking tin and fill with the mixture. Bake in a moderate oven for 45 minutes, or till firm. Remove from the tin to a plate and sprinkle parsley over the top.

Vegetarian stuffed green peppers

4 green peppers
2 dessertspoons melted butter
1 large chopped onion
3 celery stalks, chopped small
100g chopped nuts (any kind will do)

100g dry wholewheat breadcrumbs
1 large carrot, grated
1 teaspoon garlic salt
3dcl yoghurt
4 teaspoons wheatgerm

Remove the stems and seed the peppers, being careful not to break them. If they are long ones, cut them in half. Mix the butter, onion, celery, nuts, breadcrumbs, carrot and garlic salt together and then mix in the yoghurt. Put the mixture in a bowl over boiling water and cook till the mixture is hot (if it gets too dry, add some more yoghurt). Stuff the peppers with the mixture, and place them in a buttered dish. Bake in a moderate oven for about 35 minutes or till cooked. Remove from the oven, sprinkle wheatgerm over the tops of the peppers, return to the oven or grill till the wheatgerm is brown.

Vegetarian Hamburg steaks

6dcl cooked brown rice
2dcl chopped hazelnuts
   (other nuts can be used)

1 egg, lightly beaten
Oil for frying
Salt if needed

Mix the rice and nuts together and moisten with the beaten egg. Shape the mixture into little hamburgers and fry in hot oil.

Walnut loaf

250g chopped walnuts
175g cooked brown rice
100g brown breadcrumbs
2 onions, chopped finely
1 heaped tablespoon
   parsley, chopped small

1 tablespoon mixed herbs
   (thyme, lemon balm etc.)
   chopped
1 beaten egg

Mix all the ingredients together with the egg. Put into a greased pan and bake in a moderately hot oven for about 45 minutes.

VEGETABLES

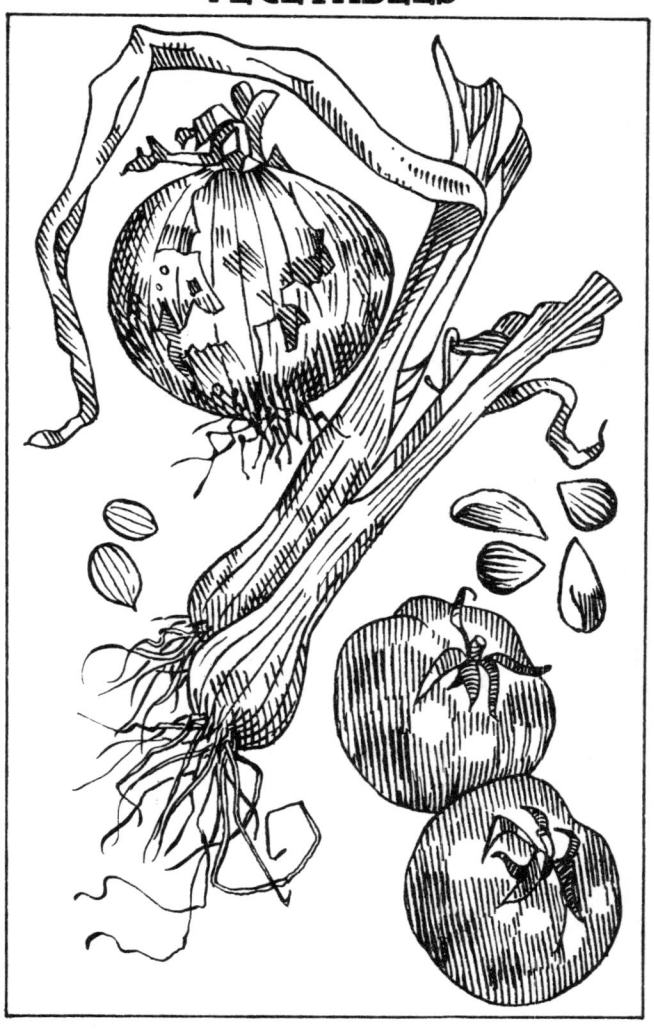

Lentils with prunes

500g lentils
500g prunes
Salt
Stock or water

Soak the lentils. Soak the prunes overnight. Cook the lentils in the salted heated stock or water till they are soft. Have the prunes ready stoned and cut into pieces. Drain the lentils and mix them with the prunes, reheat and serve with pork, goose, duck or curry.

Haricot beans can be cooked in the same way.

Spinach with rice

500g spinach
1 onion, chopped small
30g butter
1 clove garlic mashed with salt
100g brown rice (white can be used if preferred)
Juice of 1 lemon

Cook the spinach very quickly in a little boiling salted water, drain well and reserve liquid. Chop the spinach finely. Fry the onion in the butter till it is soft, then add the spinach and 5dcl of the spinach water. Stir and bring to the boil, add the garlic and rice and simmer till the rice is cooked and the water absorbed. Add the lemon juice and serve.

Brussels sprouts with chestnuts

1 teaspoon sugar
30g butter
75g cooked chestnuts
250g lightly cooked sprouts
1dcl cooking water from the sprouts
Salt

Cook the sugar in the butter till it is brown, add the chestnuts and fry gently till they are brown. Then add the sprouts, water and salt, reheat and serve.

Brussels sprouts with white grapes

250g Brussels sprouts
100g white grapes

Melted butter to taste

Boil the sprouts till cooked but not soggy. Seed the grapes and mix with the cooked sprouts, reheat and serve with melted butter poured over.

Red cabbage with apples

1 red cabbage (approx 1kg)
50g butter (oil can be
    substituted)
1 large onion chopped small

Salt, pepper
400g eating apples
100g sultanas or seedless
    raisins

Wash the cabbage and shred the leaves (discard the centre ribs if preferred). Put the butter into a pan and fry the onion gently in it till softened. Put in the cabbage, add salt and pepper and then the apples, cored and cut into quarters. Add a little water and the sultanas, cover and simmer till the cabbage is cooked. Stir from time to time and add a little water as necessary. The apples should become part of the thick sauce. Serve in the pot it was cooked in, hot or cold.

Sauerkraut with apples

6 rashers streaky bacon,
    cut into pieces
1 large onion, chopped
    small

500g sauerkraut
3dcl white stock
300g eating apples

Fry the bacon in its own fat till it begins to brown, then add the chopped onion to the bacon and simmer together till the onion is soft. Put the onion and bacon into a large pan, add the sauerkraut and the stock. Bring to the boil and simmer for about 5 minutes. Core the apples, cut them into pieces and add to the sauerkraut. Continue to simmer till the apple is soft.

Apples cooked with red cabbage

1 head of red cabbage
1 onion sliced thinly
125g fat bacon cut into
 small pieces
4 eating apples, cored and
 cut into slices

2 cloves
½ coffeespoon allspice
3 tablespoons cider vinegar
Salt and pepper

Shred the cabbage. Fry the onions with the bacon till it begins to brown, add the apples, cabbage and a little water, cover with a close fitting lid and simmer till cooked. Add the spices and vinegar, season, stir well and cook for another few minutes.

Pineapple nut rice

250g rice (brown rice is
 best)
1 large onion
50g butter
60g blanched almonds,
 roughly chopped
Salt and pepper

1 large orange
Half a large pineapple, or 1
 small one
2 hard-boiled eggs
1 heaped dessertspoon
 chopped chives

Boil the rice till just cooked, strain, rinse and drain dry. Slice the onion thinly and fry in 30g of butter with the almonds over a low heat till the onion is soft; add salt and black pepper. Now add the rice to the onion mixture and heat through. Peel the orange, remove the pith and slice, removing the pips. Skin the pineapple and cut it into pieces and fry with the orange slices in the remaining butter till golden. Put the rice into a serving dish, arrange the fruits round it and garnish with the hard-boiled eggs, cut into quarters. Scatter the chives over and serve.

Spiced bananas

4 large ripe bananas
1 coffeespoon salt
½ coffeespoon turmeric
3 tablespoons vegetable oil
3dcl coconut milk, thick if
  possible
6 large spring onions,
  chopped small, including
  green part

2cm green ginger, crushed
2 garlic cloves, crushed
1 coffeespoon fenugreek
  seeds, ground
1 teaspoon cardamom
  seeds, ground
1 teaspoon ground
  coriander
A pinch of ground nutmeg

Remove the banana skins, cut the bananas lengthwise in
halves, then cut the pieces in halves crosswise. Mix the
salt and turmeric and rub into the bananas, then fry them
in the oil. Put the coconut milk into a saucepan with the
spring onions, ginger, garlic, fenugreek, cardamom,
coriander and nutmeg, bring to the boil, reduce heat and
simmer for about 30 minutes. Then add the bananas and
continue to simmer till the sauce thickens.

Bananas with rice and vegetables

1 large garlic clove mashed
  with salt
2 onions, chopped small
50g butter
½ teaspoon turmeric
250g of rice, brown if
  possible
3 large ripe tomatoes,
  peeled and chopped small

1 red pepper, seeded and
  chopped small
1 tablespoon mixed
  chopped parsley and
  oregano
5dcl water or stock (more if
  needed)
Salt and pepper
5 ripe bananas

Fry the garlic, onions and turmeric in 20g of butter till
soft. Add the rice, stir over heat for 4 minutes then add
tomato, red pepper, herbs, stock, pepper and salt and
simmer for about 30 minutes, depending on the rice used.
When the rice is cooked but not soft, turn off the heat and

leave in the remaining water till it has been absorbed by the rice (about ½ an hour). Skin the bananas and cut them in halves lengthwise then crosswise. Fry them in the butter (the remaining 30g) then salt and pepper them and serve with the rice. Reheat if necessary.

Hot potato salad

500g potatoes
1 tablespoon chopped
   chives
1 tablespoon chopped
   parsley

Salt and pepper
1dcl olive oil plus a little
   more to oil the dish
½dcl lemon juice

Cook the potatoes in their skins in salted water till just cooked; cool, remove skins and cut into thin slices. Put a little olive oil into an ovenproof dish and put the potatoes in, sprinkling with the chives and parsley and salt and pepper. Mix the olive oil together with the lemon juice and pour over the potatoes. Cover the dish and reheat in the oven.

Tomato and apple curry

3 large cooking apples
250g tomatoes
1 large onion, chopped
   small
30g butter

1 dessertspoon curry
   powder
1½dcl stock
Salt, pepper
250g cooked rice

Core the apples and cut into pieces. Cut the tomatoes into pieces. Cook the onion in the butter till it is soft then add the curry powder and cook together, stirring for a minute or two. Add the apple and tomatoes and cook, stirring from time to time, for 10 minutes, then add the stock, salt and pepper. Bring to the boil, add the rice and simmer together for 5 minutes more.

Green beans with apples, as cooked in Slovenia

400g of green beans
Salt
750g eating apples
50g sugar (if the apples are
   sweet the sugar will not
   be necessary)

50g breadcrumbs
50g butter

Cook the beans quickly in a little salted water till they are just tender, then drain. Wash the apples, core them (but do not peel them) and cut in thick slices. Cook in a little water (and sugar, if required) till just tender; mix with the beans. Cook the breadcrumbs in the butter till they are crisp, add to the apples and beans and serve.

Green beans and lemon

500g green beans
Salt
1 tablespoon butter
1 tablespoon chopped
   parsley

Freshly ground black
   pepper
Juice of 1 lemon

Cook the beans in boiling salted water till just tender, drain and rinse in cold water. Melt the butter and add the beans, parsley and pepper and simmer together for 5 minutes. Just before serving add the lemon juice.

Green beans with pears

750g green beans
4dcl white stock
500g pears

Salt, pepper
The juice of ½ a lemon

Cut the beans into pieces about 3cm long. Put them into a saucepan and pour heated stock over them. Boil for ten minutes, then add the pears, cored and cut into quarters. Cook over a low heat till pears and beans are tender, add pepper and salt to taste and the juice of half a lemon. If preferred, the sauce (i.e. the stock in which the beans and pears were cooked) can be thickened with 1 tablespoon of flour fried in 30g of butter.

Courgettes with peanuts

1kg courgettes	30g butter
250g shelled peanuts, roasted	Salt, pepper

Cook the courgettes fast in boiling salted water. Drain and chop very small. Chop the peanuts small, melt the butter and mix peanuts, courgettes and the butter together, add salt and pepper to taste and serve.

Coconut curry

1 coconut	1 coffeespoon paprika
1 dessertspoon lemon juice	pepper
1 large onion, grated	2 large onions, sliced thinly
50g butter	1 coffeespoon salt
½ coffeespoon turmeric	6 hard-boiled eggs sliced
½ dessertspoon ground coriander	thickly

Remove the coconut flesh from the shell, reserve the liquid and grate the flesh finely. Mix the coconut with the lemon juice. Fry the grated onion in the butter with the turmeric, coriander and paprika till the onion is soft and a nice brown colour. Add the coconut and cook for about 5 minutes, then add the sliced onion and fry for a few minutes more. Pour in the liquid from the coconut gradually, stirring gently all the time, add the salt and simmer for about 15 minutes. Put the coconut in a dish and top with the hard-boiled egg slices.

Cold marinated leeks

750g leeks
Stock
4 garlic cloves, crushed in salt
The rind of half a lemon
½ coffeespoon grated nutmeg
½ teaspoon ground cinnamon
1 bay leaf

A pinch of turmeric (rather less than ¼ of a coffee-spoon)
3 tablespoons vegetable oil (sunflower oil is best)
The juice of 2 lemons
1 teaspoon salt
½ coffeespoon black pepper
30g butter
30g flour

Wash the leeks well and remove any dirty outer leaves but leave whole. Put enough stock into a large shallow pan just to cover the leeks, add the garlic, lemon rind, nutmeg, cinnamon, bay leaf, turmeric, and half the salt. Cover the pan, bring to the boil, reduce the heat and simmer till the leeks are cooked, about 20 minutes. Drain the leeks and press them gently to remove liquid from them. Reserve the liquid. Mix the oil, lemon juice, black pepper and a little salt together. Prick the leeks all over with a fork and put into a dish, pour the marinade over and leave for 6 or 7 hours.

Before eating make a sauce from the butter, flour and stock the leeks were cooked in.

Prune and date ražnjići

250g big prunes
2 bay leaves
250g large dates
1dcl walnuts
Butter to fry nuts

Spiced rhubarb as needed (see recipe on p. 123)
250g streaky bacon (thinly sliced)
4 eating apples

Pour boiling water over the prunes and leave them to soak overnight with the bay leaves. If they are not soft by the next day, simmer them in the water till tender. Stone the prunes and the dates. Chop the nuts and fry them for a few minutes in a little butter, then mix enough rhubarb to bind them together. Fill the dates and prunes with the mixture and wrap a piece of the bacon around each one. Core the apples and cut them into pieces about the size of the bacon-wrapped fruits. Thread on skewers: prune, apple slice, date, apple slice, prune, and so on. Grill the ražnjići and serve with rice and salad.

Yellow rice

250g rice	5dcl water
30g butter	1 teaspoon salt
1 teaspoon turmeric	100g raisins, seedless

Wash the rice. Put the butter into a pan, add the turmeric and stir over a medium heat for about 3 minutes. Add the rice and stir till the grains look glassy. Add the water, heated to boiling point, the salt and raisins and simmer until the rice is cooked – the time will depend on the rice used (white rice will take about ½ an hour, brown rice will take longer).

Rice with chestnuts

4 stalks celery	1 dessertspoon oregano,
Stock (about 6dcl)	chopped small
250g rice (brown is best for this)	Salt, pepper
	30g butter
250g shelled chestnuts	

Cut the celery into pieces and cook in the stock till tender. Put into a blender or through a mouligrater. Put the rice and chestnuts into a pan with the oregano, salt and pepper to taste (this depends on the stock) and the stock (there should be enough to cover the rice and chestnuts). Add the butter and bring to the boil, then lower the heat and simmer till chestnuts and rice are cooked and the stock absorbed. This will take about 40 minutes, depending on the rice used.

Rice with nuts and apricots

2 sliced onions
50g butter
2 garlic cloves
2cm green ginger
1 coffeespoon turmeric
250g rice
Stock (double the volume of
    rice)

Salt, pepper
200g fresh apricots, stoned
50g blanched almonds
50g stoned grapes
2dcl yoghurt

Fry the onions in the butter, add the garlic and green ginger thinly sliced, and the turmeric and fry together for a few minutes. Then add the rice, enough stock or water to cover the rice, and salt and pepper. Simmer till the rice is almost cooked, adding water if needed. Add the halved stoned apricots, the almonds chopped in fairly large pieces, the grapes and the yoghurt, stir together, reheat and serve.

Rice with nuts

250g rice
2dcl tomato juice
1 dessertspoon chopped
    fresh tarragon (or 1
    coffeespoon if dried)

Salt, pepper
250g mixed chopped nuts
30g butter

Cook the rice till it is just tender; do not overcook it. Heat the tomato juice with the tarragon and salt and pepper. Grease an oven dish and put a layer of rice on to it, then a layer of nuts, and continue till the rice and nuts are used up. Pour the tomato juice over the top to cover completely. Put little pieces of butter over the top and bake in a hot oven for about 20 minutes.

Rice as cooked in Iraq

3dcl rice
125g almonds, skinned and
  cut into very thin slices

200g currants
125g candied orange peel
¾dcl sunflower oil

Cook the rice till soft but firm, then drain. Mix together
the almonds, currants and peel. In an oven dish put a
layer of rice, top with a layer of peel, almonds and
currants; repeat twice more so that there are three layers
of each. Pour the oil over the top, cover with a tight fitting
lid and put back in a very low oven for 2 hours. This rice
dish is good served with lamb.

BREADS, CAKES AND DESSERTS

Apple kuchen

150g butter
60g sugar
1 small coffeespoon salt
3dcl boiled milk
30g fresh yeast or ½ packet
   dried yeast dissolved in
   ¾dcl warm water

2 egg yolks, well beaten
500g flour
30g melted butter
500g cooking apples
100g sugar
1 coffeespoon freshly
   ground cinnamon
100g seedless raisins

Put the butter, sugar and salt into the hot milk, cool, and
when lukewarm add the yeast, egg and sufficient flour to
make a stiff batter. Cover and allow to rise until the dough
has doubled in bulk. Then cut it down and beat it well. Put
into two buttered cake tins and brush over with melted
butter.

Core and peel the apples and cut them into eighths;
press the sharp edges into the dough. Mix the sugar with
the cinnamon and raisins and sprinkle over the top of the
apples. Cover and allow to rise again. Bake for about half
an hour in a moderate oven.

Nut and date bread

200g dates, chopped small
1½dcl honey
1dcl (scant) melted butter
2dcl boiling water
1 egg
100g chopped nuts (any
   kind will do)

375g plain flour
1 teaspoon bicarbonate of
   soda
1 coffeespoon salt

Mix the dates, honey, butter and water together. Cool,
then add the egg, well beaten, the nuts and the flour
mixed with the bicarbonate of soda and salt. Mix all well
together and bake in a moderate oven in a buttered tin for
about 45 minutes.

Wholewheat nut bread

200g brown sugar
2dcl water
150g molasses
2dcl milk
150g white flour
300g wholewheat flour

2½ teaspoons baking powder
1 teaspoon salt
1 coffeespoon bicarbonate of soda
200g chopped walnuts

Dissolve the sugar in the water, mix in the molasses and milk. Mix the flours, baking powder, salt and bicarbonate of soda together, then stir in the liquid. Add the nuts, put into a greased tin and bake in a moderate oven for about 1½ hours.

Slovenian potica

35g yeast plus 2 tablespoons tepid milk and a soupspoon of honey to make leaven
1 egg
100g butter

50g sugar
Grated peel of 1 lemon
3dcl milk (more if needed)
600g flour
1 small coffeespoon salt

Crumble the yeast into the warm milk and honey and put in a warm place to ferment. Beat the egg, butter and sugar together till thick and creamy, add the lemon peel and the warmed milk and then the flour, salt and yeast milk. Beat the mixture together with the hand till the dough comes away cleanly from the mixing bowl and hands. Cover the bowl with a cloth and put in a warm place to rise.

When the dough has doubled in bulk, roll it out to the thickness of your middle finger on a floured board. Spread the filling (see below) over the dough and roll up like a Swiss roll. Have ready one or two loaf tins, well greased. Put the dough into them and put in a warm place to prove. Brush over with beaten egg and bake in a hot oven for about an hour (depending on the size of tins or tin used).

Use one of the following fillings.

Almond filling

300g ground almonds
150g sugar
2 eggs
100g butter

The grated rind of 1 lemon
1½dcl thick cream
50g seedless sultanas

Grind the almonds roughly and heat them with 75g of the sugar till the sugar begins to turn yellow. Cool. When cold, beat the eggs with the remaining sugar, butter and lemon peel and add to the sugar and almonds. Stir in the sultanas then add the cream slowly. The mixture must be thick enough to spread.

Chocolate almond filling

4 eggs, separated
50g sugar
200g butter

250g plain chocolate
250g ground almonds

Mix the egg yolks and sugar till a light lemon colour, add the softened butter and mix well together. Add the chocolate either grated or melted over boiling water. Beat the egg whites stiff and fold in. Spread this mixture over the dough, scatter the ground almonds over and roll up.

Cocoa and walnut filling

200g vanilla flavoured
  sugar
400g ground walnuts (or
  150g ground walnuts and
  2 bread rolls made into
  fine crumbs)
1 tablespoon cocoa

The grated rind of 1 lemon
¾ teaspoon ground
  cinnamon
20g butter
Cream as needed
50g chopped walnuts

Mix the sugar and ground nuts together, add the cocoa, lemon peel, cinnamon and butter (just melted). Mix together till smooth with the cream. Spread over the dough, scatter the chopped walnuts over and roll up.

103

Apricot and almond flavoured bread

4dcl boiling water
100g dried apricots,
    chopped in small pieces
2 tablespoons butter
1 teaspoon salt
225g sugar

1 egg, well beaten
150g wholewheat flour
200g plain white flour
1 teaspoon bicarbonate of
    soda
200g chopped almonds

Pour the water over the apricots, add the butter, salt and sugar and cool. Then add the other ingredients and mix well together. Butter a bread tin and put the mixture into it. Bake in a moderate oven for about 1½ hours.

Banana bread

3 large ripe bananas
2 eggs, beaten till very
    light
150g sugar
300g flour

1 teaspoon salt
1 teaspoon bicarbonate of
    soda
150g chopped hazelnuts (or
    other nuts)

Crush the bananas, add the eggs to them and the sugar, flour, salt, bicarbonate of soda and nuts. Mix well together and put into a greased pan. Bake in a moderate oven for about an hour.

Orange peel bread

200g orange peel, cut into
    small pieces (first remove
    the pith)
375g sugar
30g butter

6dcl milk
1 egg
600g flour
4 teaspoons baking powder
Pinch of salt

Cover the pieces of orange peel with water and bring to the boil, then cook, simmering, till the peel is soft. Drain the peel and add 180g of the sugar to the water. Boil till a syrup forms. Cream the butter with the remaining sugar, add the milk, egg and flour and mix thoroughly together with the baking powder and salt. Now add the orange peel and mix in. Have ready a large buttered pan, put the mixture into it. Leave to rise for 30 minutes, then bake in a low oven for about 45 minutes.

Prune bread

2 tablespoons melted butter
225g sugar
300g prunes, cooked, stoned and cut into pieces
1 egg
3dcl liquid the prunes were cooked in
1 teaspoon bicarbonate of soda

3dcl sour milk
150g wholewheat flour
150g plain white flour
1 small coffeespoon baking powder
1 small coffeespoon salt

Mix together the butter, sugar, prunes, egg and prune juice. Mix the bicarbonate of soda with the sour milk and stir into the prune mixture. Sift the wholewheat flour, white flour, baking powder and salt together and add to the other ingredients; beat together till well blended. Bake in a greased tin in a moderate oven for about 1 hour.

Apple cake

6 eggs, separated
6 tablespoons sugar
6 tablespoons flour

500g eating apples, cored and cut into thin slices

Beat the egg whites stiff, add the sugar little by little and then the egg yolks, well beaten. Fold in the flour and the apple slices. Butter and flour a large cake tin and fill it with the apple cake mixture. Bake in a fairly hot oven for about 40 minutes. Cool the cake and cut into squares. Sprinkle the tops with a little castor sugar.

Blackcurrant cake

Pastry
300g flour
150g butter
70g sugar

40g almonds
2 egg yolks
The grated rind of 1 lemon

Filling
500g blackcurrants
30g sugar
Cornflour to thicken

1dcl blackcurrant jam
2dcl sweetened cream

Make a pastry with the flour, butter, sugar and the almonds, ground finely, the lemon peel and egg yolks. Line a large flan case with the pastry and bake blind.

Put the cleaned blackcurrants in a bowl with the sugar. Place over a pan of boiling water and cook them till the juices run. Thicken with a little cornflour and allow to cool.

Put a little jam on the bottom of the cooked flan case, fill with the blackcurrants, put a little more jam on top and serve with the cream, whipped lightly.

Nut cake

100g butter
4 eggs, separated
200g sugar
200g hazelnuts, almonds or
    walnuts, ground

2 tablespoons cocoa
The grated rind of 1 orange
The juice of 1 lemon

Icing and filling
3dcl whipping cream
100g plain chocolate,
    melted

2 tablespoons powdered
    sugar

Beat the butter till it is light and soft, add the yolks of egg, one by one, beating gently till they are well blended with the butter, then add the sugar and beat till the mixture is creamy and light. Add the ground nuts, cocoa, orange peel and lemon juice, beat the egg whites stiff and fold into the cake mixture. Bake in a well greased tin at a moderate heat.

To make the icing and filling, whip the cream and the melted chocolate with the powdered sugar. When the cake is cool, cut in half, fill with half the chocolate mixture, and ice with the remaining chocolate mixture.

White of egg cake with lemon cream filling

6 egg whites
A pinch of salt
1 teaspoon baking powder
300g vanilla flavoured
    sugar

2 teaspoons cider vinegar
2 teaspoons water

Cream filling
7 level tablespoons
    cornflour
150g sugar
A pinch of salt
7½dcl milk

6 egg yolks
1½dcl lemon juice
The grated rind of 1 lemon
2½dcl cream

Whip the egg whites with the salt and baking powder, beat in the sugar, then the vinegar and water and continue beating till the mixture is stiff and shiny. Grease a large round cake tin, put the mixture into it and bake in a slow oven for about 1½ hours. Cool the cake in the tin and remove when cold.

To make the filling, mix the cornflour, sugar and salt in a pan, add the milk slowly, mixing well, and heat over a low flame until the mixture is well blended and smooth. Beat the egg yolks in and then cook over hot water till the mixture thickens. Remove from the heat, add the lemon juice and rind, mix well and then leave to cool.

Four hours before serving, whip the cream lightly, fold it into the lemon cream and cover the cake with this mixture. Put into the refrigerator to set.

Chestnut cake

1kg cooked, sieved
   chestnuts
6 eggs, separated

500g vanilla-flavoured
   sugar

Icing
100g butter
125g melted chocolate
4 egg yolks

Ground walnuts
10 walnut halves

Put the chestnut purée, egg yolks and sugar into a large bowl and beat together. Beat the egg whites stiff and fold in. Put the mixture into a greased, floured tin and bake in a moderate oven for about an hour.

To make the topping, soften the butter and mix together with the melted chocolate in a large bowl. Add the egg yolks, stirring well. Put the bowl over a pan of boiling water and beat gently till the mixture thickens. Cool the cake and then ice with the mixture, spreading it over the top and down the sides. Scatter ground walnuts over the top and decorate with the walnut halves.

Schaum torta

250g crushed pineapple
250g mashed strawberries
1 tablespoon orange
   liqueur, if available
8 egg whites

250g white sugar
1 tablespoon lemon juice
3dcl whipped cream
12 whole strawberries

Mix the pineapple, strawberries and orange liqueur together and leave in a cold place until needed.

Put the egg whites into a bowl and beat them stiff. Add the sugar to them little by little, beating all the time. After half the sugar has been added, start to add some lemon juice with each amount of sugar, and continue till all the sugar and lemon juice have been used up. Put this meringue mixture into a large greased cake tin with a removable bottom and bake in a very slow oven for about an hour. Then open the oven door and cook for 30 minutes more, then turn the oven off and leave the cake inside until the oven is cold.

Take the meringue out of its tin and split into two halves. Leave to cool. When cold, spread the bottom half with the strawberry and pineapple mixture and top with whipped cream. Cover with the second half of the cake and decorate the top with whole strawberries.

Orange cake

4 eggs, separated
120g sugar
The grated rind of 1 orange
120g ground almonds

60g dried breadcrumbs soaked in the juice of 3 oranges

Mix the egg yolks with the sugar till smooth and lemon-coloured, add the grated orange rind and then the orange-soaked breadcrumbs and ground almonds. Beat the egg whites stiff and fold into the mixture. Put into a greased, floured tin and bake in a moderate oven for about 1 hour, or till the sides of the cake come away from the side of the tin.

Cherry sponge

180g butter
300g sugar
3 eggs, separated

The grated rind of 1 lemon
450g flour
1kg ripe cherries, stoned

Mix the butter with the sugar till the mixture is light and creamy. Beat the yolks into the mixture one at a time, then add the lemon rind. Mix in the flour, beat the egg whites stiff and fold into the sponge mixture. Put the mixture into a greased floured baking tin. On the top put the stoned cherries. Bake in a moderate oven for 30 minutes, then turn up the heat and bake for another 15 minutes.

Walnut Swiss roll

6 eggs, separated
160g sugar
120g walnuts

30g flour
Jam and sugar

Beat the egg yolks and sugar together till the mixture is light and lemon coloured. Grind the walnuts finely and add them with the flour, then beat the egg whites stiff and fold them into the mixture. Fill a Swiss roll tin and bake in a moderate oven. When cooked, turn out, spread with jam and roll up. Sprinkle the top with sugar.

Apple flan

Pastry
250g flour
150g butter

1 whole egg, beaten lightly
A little cold water if needed

Filling
500g eating apples
1 tablespoon sponge biscuit crumbs
1½dcl apple jelly or jam

3 cloves, ground
¼ small nutmeg, ground
2cm stick cinnamon, ground

To make the pastry, sieve the flour into a basin, rub in the butter, then mix in the egg. If the pastry is not wet enough (it should be medium firm) add a little cold water. Put in a cold place for 30 minutes. After this time line a greased and floured tin with half the pastry.

Peel all but two of the apples (or leave the peel on if you prefer) and then grate or slice them very thinly. Scatter the crumbs over the bottom of the pastry, then put the apple over them. Heat the apple jelly a little and mix in the spices; pour half of this over the apple. Core and cut the remaining apples into thin slices and arrange on top of the grated apple, then pour the rest of the jelly on. Roll out the remaining pastry to make a crust for the pie, place on top and bake in a moderately hot oven for 45 minutes.

You can also cook the pie without a top crust and use the remaining pastry for another pie shell.

Cherry flan

Pastry (see recipe on p. 116)
500g sweet cherries, stoned
45g ground hazelnuts
The grated rind of 1 lemon
¼ coffeespoon ground cinnamon

2 level teaspoons dried breadcrumbs or sponge biscuit crumbs

Make the pastry and leave it to rest. Mix the cherries with the nuts, lemon peel and cinnamon. Line a flan case with the pastry, scatter one teaspoon of crumbs over the bottom, then fill the pastry case with the cherry mixture, scatter the remaining crumbs over the top and bake in a moderate oven till cooked. This will take about an hour.

Hazelnut pie

Pastry
100g butter
160g flour
Pinch of salt

2 tablespoons cream
1 egg yolk

Filling
200g sugar
5 eggs, separated

200g ground hazelnuts
The grated rind of 1 orange

Rub the butter into the flour with a pinch of salt, add the cream and egg yolk and mix well. Grease and flour a baking sheet and roll out the pastry to fit it.

Make the filling by mixing the egg yolks and sugar together till lemon coloured and light. Add the orange peel, the nuts and the egg whites, beaten stiff.

Spread the mixture over the pastry and bake in a moderate oven till golden brown.

Walnut flan

Pastry

300g plain flour
150g softened unsalted
  butter

1 egg yolk
2 or 3 tablespoons thin
  cream as needed

Filling

3 eggs, separated
75g sugar
75g plain chocolate
Juice and grated rind of 1
  lemon

50g ground walnuts
25g chopped walnuts

To make the pastry put the flour into a bowl, make a hollow in the centre, put the butter into it with the egg and mix into the flour; add sufficient cream to make a medium soft pastry. Put the pastry in a cold place for 30 minutes.

Prepare the filling. Mix the egg yolks and sugar together, melt the chocolate and add it to the sugar and egg. Add the grated lemon rind, lemon juice and the ground and chopped walnuts. Beat the egg whites stiff and fold into the mixture. Line a flan tin with the pastry, fill with the mixture and bake in a moderate oven till the filling is firm.

You can use other nuts instead of walnuts if you prefer.

Orange and almond pudding

70g butter
70g sugar
4 eggs, separated
The grated rind of 1 orange

The juice of 1 large orange
60g fresh white
  breadcrumbs
70g grated almonds

Mix the butter, sugar and egg yolks together till all the sugar has been absorbed and the mixture has a light colour and texture. Add the orange rind, orange juice, breadcrumbs and almonds to the mixture, mix together till well blended. Beat the egg whites stiff and fold into the mixture. Have ready a mould or pudding basin greased with butter. Put the mixture into it, cover tightly and steam for about 45 minutes.

This pudding is very good served with the punch sauce on page 124, or you can serve it with fresh orange juice, either cold or heated.

Hot baked lemon pudding

1dcl flour
3dcl sugar
3 eggs, separated

1dcl lemon juice and the grated rind of 1 lemon
4½dcl milk or sour milk

Mix the flour and the sugar. Blend the egg yolks with the lemon juice, rind and milk and mix well with the flour and sugar, beating till smooth. Beat the egg whites stiff and fold them into the mixture. Butter and flour a shallow pan, fill it with the mixture and bake in a moderate oven in a dish of hot water for about 45 minutes.

Apricot soufflé

300g dried apricots
5 egg whites
100g brown sugar, crushed till it has the texture of icing sugar (this can be done very easily in an electric grinder)

Soak the apricots till they are soft, cook them and make them into a purée. Beat the egg whites till stiff and fold the sugar into them, then fold into the apricot purée. Put into a greased baking dish and cook in a cool oven till just firm.

Walnut pudding

50g butter
2½dcl milk
100g flour
4 eggs, separated
175g sugar

75g walnuts, chopped
150g apricot purée
Honey to sweeten the
    apricots

Put the butter and milk into a pan and bring to the boil. Remove from the heat and mix the flour in, little by little. Cook over a low heat till the mixture thickens. Cool, then add the egg yolks, beating them in one by one, and then 100g of the sugar. Beat the egg whites stiff and fold the nuts into them, then the remaining 75g of sugar. Fold this mixture into the flour and milk mixture. Put into a buttered mould (the mould should not be more than two-thirds full), cover with foil, place the mould in a dish of hot water and cook in a hot oven for about 30 minutes.

When cooked, turn out on to a dish and serve with the apricot purée sweetened with honey. The purée can be heated if preferred.

Hazelnuts can be used instead of walnuts, and the fruit purée can be made from damsons, plums, greengages, etc.

Pancakes

To make approximately 12 pancakes
150g flour
10g sugar
2dcl of milk

1 egg
1 tablespoon oil

Put the flour into a large bowl and add the sugar. Beat the egg and oil together, beat in the milk, then stir this liquid into the flour and beat until the batter is light and smooth.

Grease a thick pan with butter and oil, heat and when hot pour a ladle of batter into the pan. Cook till the underside is golden, then turn and cook the other side. Stack the pancakes on a warm plate and keep hot, with a teaspoon of melted butter between each pancake.

Pancakes in orange juice

2dcl orange juice (fresh, frozen or tinned, but not sweetened)

1 tablespoon grated orange peel
1½dcl golden syrup or honey

Put the orange juice, peel and syrup or honey in a bowl and let them stand for about an hour in a warm place. Dip each pancake into the juice and put them into an oven-proof serving dish (a round one the size of the pancakes is best). Pour the remaining juice over them and bake in a hot oven till all are well heated.

Pancakes with strawberries and cream

500g strawberries
The grated rind of 1 lemon

Powdered sugar as needed

Mix the strawberries with the lemon peel and sugar to taste. Set aside to allow the sugar to be absorbed by the fruit. Make the pancakes, fill with the strawberry mixture and roll up.

These pancakes can be served hot by heating the strawberry mixture before filling. They are also very good if the pancakes are hot and the filling cold, served with whipped cream.

Pancakes with walnuts

3dcl cream
100g finely chopped or ground walnuts
1 tablespoon coarsely chopped walnuts

1 heaped tablespoon thick honey

Whip the cream, add the nuts with the honey and fill the pancakes with the mixture.

Almond pastry

250g butter
250g ground sugar
1 egg

250g almonds
250g flour

Soften the butter, add the sugar to it and mix well till smooth and creamy. Add the egg and mix it in well, then add the almonds and flour. Mix into a pastry. Put in a cold place for 30 minutes before rolling out thinly.

This is a very tasty pastry. Use it for fruit flans.

Sherbert ice cream

3dcl whipping cream
1½dcl unsweetened fruit
juice

1dcl honey
2 egg whites

Whip the cream lightly and mix with the fruit juice. Add the honey slowly and mix together. Put into a container and freeze till firm. Then put the mixture into a bowl and beat till smooth in texture. Beat the egg whites stiff and fold into the fruit and cream. Put into a container and re-freeze.

Pineapple sherbert

1 pineapple, enough to
provide 5dcl of grated
fruit
½ packet gelatine
The juice of 2 lemons

375g brown sugar, ground
fine like icing sugar (use
less if the fruit is very
sweet)

Remove the skin from the pineapple and grate the fruit. Heat to boiling point, remove from the heat. Dissolve the gelatine in 2½dcl of water, add it to the pineapple, then add the lemon juice and sugar. Mix all well together and freeze.

Strawberry ice cream

500g strawberries
2 tablespoons castor sugar
(or more, or less,
depending on the
sweetness of the fruit)

3dcl cream, lightly whipped

Crush the strawberries with the sugar and mix with the whipped cream. Put into containers and freeze.

Raspberries, peaches or other fruit can be used instead of strawberries.

Pineapple custard

1 small pineapple
2½dcl syrup

4 eggs
5dcl milk

Remove the skin from the pineapple and grate the flesh. Mix 2dcl of pineapple pulp with the syrup and simmer for about 5 minutes, then cool. When cold, beat the eggs and then beat them into the pineapple syrup. Stir the milk into the mixture, put it into an oven dish and bake in a moderate oven till the custard sets. Serve hot or cold.

Fruit yoghurt sherbert

3dcl thick yoghurt
1½dcl raspberry juice (or
other fruit juice)

1dcl honey
2 egg whites

Mix the yoghurt and fruit juice together with the honey in a blender. Put into a container and freeze. When frozen, remove from the container, put into a large bowl and beat till smooth. Beat the egg whites stiff and fold them into the fruit mixture. Replace in the container and refreeze.

Light lemon mousse

1 packet gelatine
1½dcl honey
The juice of 3 lemons, the
    grated rind of 2
Water (enough to make up
    the amount of lemon
    juice to 5½dcl)

2dcl whipping cream
3 egg whites

Put the gelatine into a cup with 1dcl of water, mix and leave for about 10 minutes to dissolve. Heat the remaining water with the honey, bring to boiling point, remove from the heat and stir into the dissolved gelatine. When thoroughly blended, add the lemon juice and grated rind and mix together. Leave to cool. When the mixture is cold, whip the cream, fold in and put in the refrigerator. When the jelly is beginning to set, whip the egg whites and fold into the jelly. Put into the refrigerator to set completely.

Apple cream

500g eating apples
20g butter
A piece of vanilla pod
1dcl water
75g honey
1dcl syrup made from sugar
    and water, medium thick

2dcl whipped cream (not
    whipped too stiffly)
1 dessertspoon chopped
    almonds or hazelnuts
15g powdered sugar

Peel 375g of the apples, core them and slice them thinly. Put them in a pan with the butter, vanilla and water, cover closely and simmer till they are mushy, then remove the lid and stir over a moderate heat till all the liquid has evaporated. Add the honey and stir well, remove the vanilla pod and leave to cool.

Peel the remaining apples, cut them into quarters, remove the cores and then cut each quarter in two. Poach these apple pieces carefully in the syrup (they must remain whole), then drain and cool them.

Mix the cooled apple purée with the whipped cream and put in the refrigerator for about 2 hours. Decorate the top before serving by sprinkling the nuts over, then arrange the apple slices over the nuts and scatter powdered sugar over the whole.

Chilled apricot cream

200g dried apricots, soaked, cooked and drained

3dcl yoghurt
1dcl honey

Pulp the apricots in a blender or by passing them through a sieve. Mix them with the yoghurt, add the honey and mix well together. Put into a container and chill.

Fruit cream

250g fruit (any fruit can be used – apricots, peaches, plums, berries, etc)
Honey (the amount will depend on the fruit you use. Between 1 and 2dcl should be enough)

1 packet gelatine
A little water
1½dcl cream, lightly whipped
1 egg white

Remove the stones from the fruit if necessary, and if they are hard fruit, stew them till soft (berries do not need cooking). Sieve or crush the fruit, put into a pan and heat but do not boil. Dissolve the gelatine in a little water, then mix with the fruit and allow to cool. When cold, mix the lightly whipped cream into the fruit, put into the refrigerator and leave there till the cream is beginning to set. Beat the egg white stiff and fold into the cream. Put back into the refrigerator until completely set.

Orange salad

8 ripe thin-skinned oranges
Powdered brown sugar as
  needed
1 small glass orange
  liqueur if available

Candied orange peel to
  garnish

Peel the oranges, remove the pith with a potato peeler, then slice the oranges crossways thinly into a bowl. Add sugar (the amount you need will depend on the sweetness of the oranges), and if available, pour over a glass of orange liqueur. Garnish with little slices of candied orange peel.

Fresh figs with cream

250g figs
The juice of 1 lime

3dcl whipped cream

Cut the figs into quarters, sprinkle with lime juice and mix with the cream.

Dates in honey and cream

20 large dates
30g blanched almonds
1 tablespoon grated orange
  rind
2 tablespoons maraschino
  liqueur or other cherry
  brandy

1dcl warmed honey
3dcl very cold thick cream

Remove the stones from the dates. Grind the almonds and mix with the orange rind and maraschino. Stuff the dates with this mixture, put them into a bowl, pour the honey and then the cream over them and chill before serving.

Oatmeal with prunes

8dcl milk (sour milk is best)
250g oatmeal
Salt

250g prunes (these should
  not be too dry), stoned
1dcl cream

Bring the milk to the boil, sprinkle in the oatmeal, add a little salt and simmer till smooth. This will take about 45 minutes. Half way through the cooking add the prunes. Just before serving, pour the cream over.

Orange perfection

12 thin-skinned oranges
2 litres water
1kg sugar

1 stick vanilla
3 cloves
Orange liqueur

Wash the oranges thoroughly. Scrape the orange skins to roughen them – do not cut too deeply into them. Cut the oranges from 1cm from the top to the bottom, five or six times, making sure that the cut goes right through the skin but not deep into the orange.

Make a thin syrup with the water, sugar and spices. Simmer the oranges in the syrup for about 2 hours till it becomes jellified and each orange is just covered by syrup. Allow to cool, then take each orange and press it between your thumb and first finger so that the fingers almost come together. Put the oranges in a dish and pour over the syrup with orange liqueur added to it.

You can eat these immediately or keep them in a jar for some weeks.

JELLIES, SAUCES AND STUFFINGS

Apple jelly

2kg cooking apples (crab apples are also good)

Water
Sugar

Put the apples into a large pan, cut into pieces but not skinned or cored. Add just enough water to cover, bring to the boil, cover and boil till the fruit is mushy. Strain through a muslin or preferably a linen cloth. Do not squeeze the cloth or the jelly will be cloudy.

Measure the amount of juice and add the same volume of sugar. Boil together until the jelly sets when a little is put on to a plate. The time depends on the type of apple used. Skim off any scum on the top of the jelly, fill clean heated glass jars, cool and seal.

Very good mint jelly can be made using apple jelly and fresh mint. Cook chopped mint leaves with the apple jelly (9dcl of juice to 3dcl of chopped leaves).

The following fruits can be made into fruit jelly in the same way; they too are rich in pectin: sour blackberries, gooseberries, lemons, grapefruits, sour oranges, plums, loganberries.

Spiced rhubarb

1kg rhubarb
2 lemons
4 large cloves of garlic
4cm fresh ginger

500g seedless sultanas
1kg brown sugar
6dcl cider vinegar

Wash the rhubarb and cut into small pieces. Skin the lemons, remove the pith with a potato peeler, remove the pips and cut the fruit small. Crush the garlic and the ginger. Put all the ingredients into a pan, bring to the boil and cook till the mixture is thick. Put into heated bottles, cover and keep for 2 weeks before using.

(If you have a blender, use it to crush the garlic and ginger, moistened with a little of the vinegar.)

Dalmatian caper sauce

2dcl olive oil
3 large tinned sardines
1 tablespoon chopped
  parsley
3 cloves garlic mashed with
  salt

Juice of 2 lemons
1 tablespoon chopped
  capers
Freshly ground black
  pepper

Beat the oil with the sardines over a low heat till the sardines merge with the oil. Add the parsley, garlic, lemon juice, capers, pepper and, if necessary, salt. Heat together slowly to boiling point, cool and serve with cold fish, salami, etc.

Punch sauce

3 eggs
100g sugar
2dcl cold tea

3 tablespoons rum
Juice of 1 orange
Juice of ½ lemon

Mix all the ingredients together and put into a bowl over gently boiling water. Beat till the sauce is thick and frothy but do not let the sauce become too hot. Serve warm, with steamed puddings.

Lemon sauce for fish

100g breadcrumbs
100g butter
2dcl stock
Juice of 1 lemon, grated
  rind of ½ lemon

Pepper, salt
1 egg yolk

Fry the crumbs slowly in the butter till a light brown colour, add the stock and lemon rind and bring to the boil. Add the lemon juice, pepper and salt. Beat the egg yolk and pour the hot liquid on to it, beating well. Serve.

Fish sauce

The yolks of 4 hard-boiled
   eggs
3 tablespoons olive oil
2dcl fish stock
1½dcl white wine
The juice of 2 lemons

1 dessertspoon chopped
   capers
1 large pickled gherkin,
   chopped small
3 anchovies, cut up small
Salt and black pepper

Mash the yolks smooth, add the oil, stock and wine and heat together, stirring, till the mixture thickens. Add the lemon juice, capers, gherkin and anchovies and pepper and salt if necessary.

Lemon garlic sauce for grilled fish

½dcl oil (olive oil is best)
The juice of 1 large lemon
3 garlic cloves, crushed in
   salt
1 dessertspoon chopped
   lemon balm

1 teaspoon each chopped
   oregano, fennel, parsley
   (as available)
Salt, pepper

Mix the oil with the lemon juice, garlic, herbs and salt and pepper.

Orange stuffing for chicken, duck, pork, etc.

2dcl orange juice
450g bread, cut into cubes
   (wholewheat bread is
   best)
The grated rind of 1 orange
100g orange (all pith
   removed)

200g celery, chopped small
¾dcl melted butter
1 egg
Salt and pepper to taste

Heat the orange juice and soak the bread in it. When the

bread has absorbed the juice, add the rind, orange, celery, melted butter and the egg, well beaten. Mix all well together and add salt and pepper to taste.

Walnut stuffing for fish, poultry, pork, etc.

125g butter
2 celery stalks, chopped
  small
1 medium sized onion,
  chopped small
450g dried breadcrumbs
  (brown are best)
150g roughly chopped
  walnuts

1 teaspoon dried sage or 1
  dessertspoon fresh sage,
  chopped
1 level teaspoon salt
Freshly ground black
  pepper

Melt the butter in a pan large enough to take all the ingredients, add the celery and onion and fry on a low heat till they begin to brown and are soft. Remove from the heat and mix in the breadcrumbs, walnuts, sage, salt and pepper.

INDEX